James Mylne

Poems, Consisting of Miscellaneous Pieces, And Two Tragedies

.

James Mylne

Poems, Consisting of Miscellaneous Pieces, And Two Tragedies

ISBN/EAN: 9783744716994

Printed in Europe, USA, Canada, Australia, Japan

Cover: Foto ©Thomas Meinert / pixelio.de

More available books at **www.hansebooks.com**

P O E M S,

CONSISTING OF

MISCELLANEOUS PIECES,

AND

TWO TRAGEDIES.

BY THE LATE
JAMES MYLNE, AT LOCHILL.

EDINBURGH:
PRINTED FOR WILLIAM CREECH,
AND SOLD BY T. CADELL,
LONDON.

MDCCXC.

HENRY DUNDAS OF MELVILLE,

TREASURER OF THE NAVY, &c.

SIR,

WHEN I do myfelf the honour of dedicating this book to you, I only fulfil the
wifhes of a much lamented parent: For I
know well, had that modefty, which gave
his character its marked, and peculiar diftinction, ever permitted him to publifh
any thing himfelf, that he would have
fought protection for it under your name.
You, Sir, encouraged and directed his firft
poetical flights ; and, it ought to be record-
ed to your immortal honour, that, in the
high rank in which you have long ftood,

and

and amidſt a multiplicity of the moſt important national concerns, you continued to remember and love the friend of your early youth. It is not uncommon to fill the page of dedication with exaggerated praiſe: But though your character and abilities in public life afford ample ſubject for exalted panegyric, it is beyond my ſphere to write of ſuch high matters.—But the virtues which adorn your private character, as they accord with the feelings of every honeſt heart, it is the buſineſs of every honeſt heart to applaud. I know, that minds warped by prejudice, or enflamed by party, will paint the moſt honourable ſcenes of life with dark and unſeemly colouring: But, if it ever ſhall happen that you retire from that exalted ſtation, where the beſt of men are expoſed to the ſhafts of envy and faction, it will then be believed by the world, as it is at preſent known to your friends, that you are as amiable in private, as reſpectable in public life; and that

your

your intereft has been uniformly, and often fuccefsfully exerted in favour of merit
and virtue, and with a view to promote
thofe men who have proved both an advantage and ornament to their country.
That you, Sir, may preferve that attach-
ment to your Sovereign, that regard for
the conftitution, and that love for your
country, which have diftinguifhed your
paft life, and raifed you high in the efteem
of every good fubject, is the moft ardent
wifh of him, who is, with the greateft refpect and veneration,

S I R,

Your moft obedient,

and moft humble Servant,

GEORGE MYLNE.

P R E F A C E.

THE Author of the following poetical pieces lives only in the remembrance of his friends; and there he will live, as long as unaffected modesty, warm, and generous feelings, an amiable simplicity of manners, and uncorrupted integrity of heart, are regarded and cultivated among men.——His genius led him in an early period of life to poetry; and his taste in that line of composition was afterwards cultivated and improved by a regular and liberal academical education, and an acquaintance with the best ancient and modern poets.

The pieces being now at the bar of the public, the proper judge of all literary merit, it would be idle, as well as unavailing, to say any thing in their praise. To excuse, however, trivial faults, it is but just to observe, that they come into the world with all the disadvantages which can possibly attend posthumous publications; none of them having been prepared for the public eye, nor received the last corrections of the Author. They were written in the midst of many avocations, and a multiplity of family and professional concerns; and it has often been a matter of astonishment to his intimate

intimate friends, that the focial intercourfe, and real bufinefs, in which they knew he was engaged, permitted him to facrifice fo much of his time and labours to the mufes.——Had they received his laft correcting hand, they would have been lefs open to the cavils of criticifm : For, though they have been feen, and read by many gentlemen of learning and tafte, they have undergone no very material alterations or amendments. Although the minor critic, who meafures every performance with the line and compafs, may perhaps find fome fmall foundation for exercifing his fkill ; it is hoped, that the reader of feeling and tafte will be delighted with many beautiful verfes, and meet with many paffages of real poetic merit.——With refpect to their moral tendency, I am perfuaded the moft fcrupulous reader will find nothing to difguft or offend him.——The Author himfelf was a man of virtue: And to fhew " Virtue in " her own fhape how lovely;" to inculcate, the practice of it as favourable to our own felicity ; and to point out mifery and fhame as the unvaried confequences of guilt and difhonour, will, I truft, be found to be the principal and ultimate object of his writings.

LIST OF SUBSCRIBERS.

A

ANDREW Agnew, Efq. younger of Lochnain
Capt. P. Agnew
Robert Anderfon, Efq. Whiburgh
John Anderfon, Efq. Winterfield
John Anftruther, Efq. Advocate, Edinburgh
Alex. Achyndachy, Efq. do.
Jofeph Alcock, Efq. Little Brook-ftreet, London
Mr Allingham, Reigate, Surrey
Mr David Armftrong, Writer, Edinburgh
Mr William Anderfon, do.
Mr Francis Anderfon, do.
Mr William Anderfon, merchant, London
Mr John Allen, do.
Mr Robert Alburn, do.
Mr William Ainflie, do.
Mr Edward Addifon, do. 2 copies
Mrs Addifon, do. 2 do.
Mr William Annand, do. 4 do.
Mrs Adair do. 2 do.
Mifs Adair do.
Mr William Ainflie, Edinburgh, 2 copies
Mr Daniel Ainflie, do.
Mr George Anderfon, Pentcaitland

Mr Charles Afhwell, Granada, 4 copies
Mr Robert Ainflie, Begbie
Lieut. Richard Allan
Mr John Atchifon, Skirling
Mr William Atchifon, St Clements Wells, 2 copies
Mr Chriftopher Armftrong, Dalkeith
Mr Robert Atchifon, Yarrow
Mr George Atchifon, Muffelburgh
Mr James Anderfon, Dalkeith
Mr John Anderfon, Soundhope
Mr Adam Anderfon, Boll-fide
Mr Andrew Anderfon, Breackhope
Mr Thomas Anderfon, baker, Edinburgh

B

Duke of Buccleugh
Duchefs of Buccleugh
Countefs Bathurft, Apfley Houfe
Sir John Wifhart Belfches
Richard Barnes, Efq. Reigate, Surrey, 5 copies
Mrs Barnes,   do.   5 do.
Mr M. W. Barnes   do.   2 do.
Robert Blair, Efq. Solicitor General, Edinburgh, 4 do.
Andrew Buchanan, Efq. Ardenconnel
George Buchanan, Efq. Achintorley
Charles Brown, Efq. Coalfton
Hugh Buchan, Efq. Edinburgh
Mr John Bogue, writer to the fignet, Edinburgh
Thomas Beaumont, Efq. Buckland, Surry
Mr Thomas Beaumont, junior, do.
Robert Borrow, Efq. Starburgh Caftle, Suffex
Capt. Henry Ball, Pendill, Surrey
Charles Birkhead, Reigate, Surrey
Mrs Birkhead,   do.
Mrs Blunt, Hotham, Suffex
—— Blagrave, Efq. Bartlet's Buildings, London
Mifs Blagrave   do.
Mrs Bankin, Eaft Grinftead, Suffex

Mr Batten, Temple
Mr Byard,   do.
Mr Bremridge, do.
Rev. John Bodicoat, Westerham, Kent
William Bridges, Esq. Wallington, Surrey, 2 copies
Mr Brewster, Warwick Land, London
Mrs Browne, Broxbourne, Herts
Mr Bucker, London, 8 copies
Mr Henry Bucker, do, 4 do.
Mr Baring,   do. 4 do.
Mrs Baring,   do. 2 do.
Mifs Baring,   do. 2 do.
Mifs Buchan, Letham
Mr Bailie, London, 2 copies
Mrs Bailie,   do. 2 do,
Mr Bernard,   do,
Mrs Bernard,   do.
Mifs Brooke,   do.
Mr Bradley,   do.
Mr Burrel,   do.
Mr Bruce,   do.
Mr Bell,   do.
Robert Burton, Esq. M. P.
—— Brown, Esq. Curry, 2 copies
Mr Robert Burton, merchant, London, 20 copies
Mr Alexander Begbie,   do.   4 do
Mr P. Begbie,   do.
Mr William Barradaile, do.
Mr Thomas Blackhouse, do.
Mr William Bruce, Tobago, 4 copies
Mr Wilfon Birkbeck, London
Mr Jofeph Ball,   do.
Mr John Burton,   do.
Mr Charles Brown, do.
Mr Philip Barton,   do.
Rev. Patrick Bannerman, Salton, 2 copies
Rev. Dr George Barclay, Haddington
Rev. James Buchanan, do.
Mr Robert Burton,   do.
Mr James Banks,   do,

Mr John Banks, Haddington
Mr John Brown, do.
Mr James Burn, do.
James Balvaird, Efq. Edinburgh
George Burnet, Efq.
Rev. James Brown, Newbattle
Mr Andrew Begbie, Barnie Mains
Mr Alexander Begbie, do.
Mr James Begbie, Craigielaw
Mr John Begbie, Stenton
Mr Patrick Bairnsfather, Heperdean
Mr James Bairnsfather, Spittal
Mr John Brodie, Whittinghame
Mr P. Brodie, Garvald
Mr Hamilton Blake, Newbarn
Mr James Brown, junior, Edinburgh
Mr Robert Burns, Ellifland
Mr Francis Brodie, writer, Edinburgh
Mr John Bertram, Redfide
Mr Hugh Bairnsfather, Straton
Mr Alexander Briggs, Dalkieth
Mr Ebenezer Bell, do.
Mr Alexander Brown, merchant, Fifherrow
Mr Robert Brown, Murkle
Mr A. Brodie
John Buchanan, Efq. Auchlefhy
—— Begbie, Efq. Kedfburgh
Mr Alexander Brown, Linton
Mr James Brown, do.
George Burnet, Efq. Edinburgh
Mr Alexander Bruce, furgeon, Muffelburgh
Andrew Bennet, Efq. Muircroft
Mr Thomas Balantine, Craig
Mr Robert Balantine, Dryhope
Mr Walter Breadon, Fiandlefhope
Mr James Beattie, Annandale
Mr Robert Boyd, Fifherrow

C

Sir Foster Cunliffe, Baronet, Chester
Sir James Colquhoun
Robert Colt, Esq. Auldhame, 2 copies
Ronald Crawford, Esq. Frisky Hall
John Corbet, Esq. Tolcrofs
Duncan Campbell, Esq, Lochnell
Mr Creech, Edinburgh, 20 copies
William Cochrane, Esq. Muirfield
Major Spencer Cochrane
John Clerk, Esq. advocate, Edinburgh
William Craig, Esq. do.
William Campbell, Esq. Donears
Mr Archibald Campbell
Mr Castell, London, 2 copies
Mr Clay, junior, do. 2 do.
Mifs Clay,   do.
Mifs E. Clay,   do.
Mr Cabell, London
Mifs Casie, New Norfolk-street, London
Mrs Clayton, Fitsey Place, Surrey
Mifs Cater, Dorking,   do.
Mifs F. Cater, do.   do.
Mifs M. Cater. do,   do.
Mrs Chomley, Ewel,   do.
Mrs Cranston, East Grinstead, Suffex
Mrs Collins   do.
Mr Cockburn, Newington Green, Middlefex
Mr Henry Callender, London, 4 copies
Mr Robert Christie, do.   4 do.
Mr Caruthers, Cheapside, do.
Mr Carter, Lombard-street, do.
Mr Crofs, Change Walk, Chelsea
Mr Dougald Campbell, London
Rev. Dr Alexander Carlyle, Inveresk
Rev. James Craig, Currie
Rev. William Cameron, Kirknewton

Rev. Patrick Carfrae, Morham
Captain Clark, 35th regiment
Lieut. John Carfrae, Carniehaugh
Mr Thomas Carfrae, Park
Mr John Carfrae, Haddington
Rev. Hugh Cunninghame, Tranent
Mr John Cunninghame, London
Mr James Cunninghame, junior, Edinburgh
Mr James Cuninghame, Luffnefs-muir
Mr Charles Cunninghame, Luffnefs-mill
Mr James Cunninghame, Drum
Mr George Cunninghame, Haddington
Mr James Cunninghame   do.
Mr William Cunninghame, do.
Mr John Clerk, junior,   do.
Mr William Cockburn, Salton
Mr John Craig, merchant, Glafgow
Mr William Crofs,   do.
Mr Peter Cox, London
Mr John Carftairs, do.
Mr David Crichton, Dalkieth
Mr William Cooper, Libberton
Mr ——— Chancellor, Edinburgh
Mr Andrew Cuthbertfon, Penfton
Thomas Carron, Efq. Wormfton
Mr John Cunninghame, Luffnefs-mill
Mr Archibald Cochrane, Muffelburgh
Mr James Cowan, Tranent

D

Right Honourable Henry Dundas, Treafurer of the Navy,
　　12 copies
Robert Dundas, Efq. of Arnifton, 2 do.
William Dundas, counfellor at law
Mrs Dundas, Bankton
Archibald Lord Douglas of Douglas
Lady E. Drummond, London, 4 copies
Mr Drummond,   do.
Henry Drummond, Efq. do.   2 copies

Mrs H. Drummond, 2 copies
Lady Sufan Drummond, Bedford-fquare
John Drummond, Efq. do.
George Douglas, Efq. Moorplace
Mrs Douglas, Sloan-ftreet
Sir Alexander Don, Newton, 2 copies
James Dempfter, Efq. Edinburgh, 2 do.
Captain Robert Dean, Huntington
Hugh Dalrymple, Efq. North Berwick
Capt. James Dalrymple, Guards
James Dunlop, Efq. Garnkirk
Robert Dunmore, Efq. Bandalloch
Mrs Dunlop, of Dunlop
Capt. William Don, Haddington
Capt. John Douglas, Jeanfield
Mr John Dunlop, Port Glafgow
Mr William Dunbar, London
Patrick Downie, Efq. Preftonpans
Capt. William Dunlop, London, 4 copies
Mr A. Dudgeon, do.
Mr James Dunfmuir, do.
Mr Lawrence M'Dowal, Granada, 4 copies
Mr Robert Dundas, writer to the fignet, Edinburgh
Mr John Dundas, do.
Mr William Dallas, do.
Patrick Dudgeon, Efq. Eaft Craig
Mr Hay Donaldfon, Haddington
Mr Alexander Dudgeon, Edinburgh
Mr John Dudgeon, Leith
Rev. Alexander Davidfon, Stentor
Mr Charles Dudgeon, Balgone Barns
Mr James Dudgeon, Drim
Rev. Robert Douglas, Galafhiels
Mr John Dods, Myreton
Mr Alexander Dods, New-mains
Mr Gregor Drummond, Edinburgh
Mr Daniel, London
Mrs Daniel, do.
Mifs Daniel, do.
Mifs F. Daniel. do.

Mr W. Dudgeon, Dryburnford
Mr Robert Dugdeon, Edinburgh
Mr Wm. Davidson, Libberton
Mr James Dickson, Edinburgh
James Drummond, Esq. Straigeath, 2 copies
David Drummond, Esq. Duchally
James Drummond, Esq. Comrie, 2 copies
Walter Dunlop, Esq. Whitmorhall
Mr Thomas Dick, Dalkieth

E

Lord Elibank,   4 copies
Lady Elibank,   4 do.
Lady Dowager Elibank, 4 do.
Sir Frederick Eden, Bart.
Thomas Eden, Esq. London
Mrs Eden,   do.
William Elliot, Esq. Wells, 2 copies
Mrs Elliot, Reigate, Surrey, 2 do.
John Peter Elige, Ricelip, Middlesex
Rev. Thomas Ellis, Nutfield, Surrey
Hon. Henry Erskine, Dean of the faculty of Advocates
Mr William Elliot, Winnington Rig
Mr James Ewen, Edinburgh

F

Lady Elizabeth Fane, Saville-row, London
Lady Mary Fane, - -   do.
James Forbes, Esq. Percy-street,   do.
Henry Fothergill, Esq. Bedford-row, do.
Mr Frazer, London, 2 copies
Mr Farrer,   do.   4 do.
Mrs Frazer,   do.   2 do.
Mr Sam. Fish, do.
George Ferguson, Esq. Kilkerran
Alexander Falconer, Esq. Woodcock-park

Rev. James Finlayfon, Edinburgh
Rev. Walter Fisher, Cranfton
Rev. T. Finlater, Linton
Mr James Forfyth, merchant, London
Mr George Forrefter, Fisherrow
Mr James Forreft, Edinburgh
Mr Alexander Frafer, Haddington
Mr Thomas Fairbairn, do.
Mr William Fernie, do.
Mr James Forreft, do.
Mr Robert Forreft, do.
Mr Patrick Forreft, North-rigg

G

Duke of Gordon
Duchefs of Gordon
Lord Gardenfton
Sir John Grefham, Bart. Fitfey-Place, Surrey
Lady Grefham
Mifs Grefham
Mifs Gavin, Lanton
Henry Glafsford, Efq. Dougalfton
James Glafsford, Efq. Glafgow
John Grieve, Efq. Commiffioner of Excife
John Glafsford, Efq. Longniddrie
Daniel Gardner, Efq. New Bond-ftreet, London
Nathaniel Green, Efq. London
Mr Glover, Reigate, Surrey
Mrs Glover, do.
Mr Ifaac Grant, writer to the fignet, Edinburgh
Mr Charles Gordon, do.
Mr John Gordon, do.
Andrew Gray, Efq. Southfield
Peter Gardner, Efq. Edinburgh
Rev. Dr. Henry Grieve, Edinburgh
Rev. George Goldie, Atholftanefoord
Rev. James Goldie, Temple
Rev. James Grant, Libberton
Mr James Gibfon, writer, Edinburgh

Mr John Gray, merchant, Edinburgh
Mr Robert Gardner, London, 4 copies
Mr Chamberlin Goodwin, do.
Mr Henry Goodwin, do.
Mr James Gubbins, do.
Alexander Gerard, Esq. Essex-street, do.
Mr William Gillespie, Anderston
Mr Henry Gillies, Musselburgh
Mr Andrew Gray, Patcox
Mr Peter Grinton, Burdichouse
Lieut. A. B. Greenless, 18th regiment foot

H

Marquis of Huntly
Countess Hyndford
Countess Dowager Harborough, New Norfolk-street, London
Lady Heathcote, Grosvenor-square, London, 2 copies
Sir Edward Hughes, K. B. Pendil, Surrey
Lady Hughes
Robert Hudson, Esq. Lower Grosvenor-street, London, 4 copies
Mrs Hay, Newhall, 4 copies
William Hamilton, Esq. Wishaw, 2 do.
Andrew Houston, Esq. Calderhall, 2 do.
Robert Hepburn, Esq. Clerkington, 4 do.
Robert Hepburn, junior, Esq. 2 do.
Mr Samuel Hepburn, 2 do.
Sir Archibald Hope, Bart. 2 do.
Mr Holland, London, 2 do.
Mrs Hanney, do. 2 do.
John Hamilton, Esq. Pentcaitland, M. P.
James Hopkirk, Esq. Dalbeth
Col. David Hepburn, Keith
G. B. Hepburn, Esq. Smeton
John Hay, Esq. Hopes
James Hay, junior, do.
Major George Hay, Inveresk
Mr Charles Hay, merchant, Dunbar

Mr Thomas Hopkirk, merchant, Glasgow
Mr George Hobson, London
Mr David Hunter, do.
Mr Charles Hippuff, do.
Dr Alexander Hamilton, Edinburgh
Mr James Hamilton, surgeon, do.
Rev. John Hamilton, Bolton
Rev. George Hamilton, Gladsmuir, 2 copies
Robert Hay, Esq. Spott
—— Hacket, Esq.
John Home Esq. Kilduff
George Home, Esq. one of the principal Clerks of Session, Edinburgh
David Hume, Esq. advocate, Edinburgh
William Honeyman, Esq. do.
Charles Hay, Esq.   do.
Mr James Home, writer to the signet, Edinburgh
Mr James Horne, do.
Mr Daniel Hamilton, do.
Miss Mary Hart, Edinburgh
Mr George Hepburn, writer, do.
Rev. Doctor Thomas Hardie, do.
Miss Hudson, Wimpole-street, London
Mrs Horseley, Epsom, Surrey
——— Hammond, Esq. Welbeck-street, London
Mrs Hammond, do.
Stephen Hough, Esq. Tavistock-street, Bedford-square, London
Mr Hore, Inner Temple, London
Mrs Hamlin, East Grinstead, Sussex
Rev. H. Hamner, Gatton, Surrey
Duncan Harrison, Esq.
Mr Haywood, Blechingley, Surrey
Mrs Henshaw, Temple, London
Mr Hilton, East Grinstead, Sussex
Mr John Hogarth
Mr Archibald Hepburn, Hailes
Mr Thomas Howden, Hugston
Mr Robert Howden, Haddington
Mr Alexander Hislop, do. 2 copies
Mr Robert Hislop,   do.

Mr Patrick Halyburton, Haddington
Mr Robert Howden, Chaple
Mr Alexander Halyburton, writer, Edinburgh
Mr William Hall, merchant,   do.
Mr Peter Hill, bookseller   do.
Mr John Howden, Congalton-mains
Mr William Hunter, Knows
Mr John Hay, Duncan-law
Mr William Howden, surgeon ,London
Mr Walter Herriot, Dalkieth
Mr Gilbert Handaside, London
Mr Thomas Haig,   do.
Mr James Kemp Hunter, merchant, Dunbar
Mr Alexander Hall, Fisherrow
Mr Archibald Handyside, do.
Mr Robert Hunter, Melrose
Mr James Howden, Edinburgh
Mr Francis Howden, do.

J

Mrs Governor Johnstone
Arthur Jones, Esq. Priory, Reigate, Surrey
Mrs Jones   do.
Miss Jones   do.
Rev. Atthur, Iredell, Guildford, Surrey
Mr Jackson, Temple
Mr Charles Innes, writer to the signet, Edinburgh
Mr William Inglis, do.
Mr Geo. Jeffrey, writer, Edinburgh
Mr James Jackson, merchant, Edinburgh
Mr Thomas Jamieson, merchant, London
Mr William Jobson   do.
Mr William Jamieson,   do.
Mr Neil Jamieson,   do. 4 copies
Mr George Jackson,   do.
Mr Alexander Innes, Edinburgh
Mr James Johnstone, Haddington
Rev. Andrew Johnstone
Mr James Johnston, Newton

Mr Alexander Johnſtone, Dunbar
Mr Samuel Johnſtone, Niddry
Mr Jackſon, London, 4 copies
Mrs Jackſon, do. 2 do.
Mr T. Jackſon, do. 2 do.
Mr. W. Jackſon, do. 2 do.
Mr Johnſon,   do. 2 do.

K

Sir David Kinloch, Gilmerton
Miſs Kinloch,   do.
Francis Kinloch, Eſq. do. 2 copies
Capt. David Kinloch, do.
Major A. Gordon Kinloch, do.
Capt. Alexander Kinloch, do.
John Kenrick, Eſq. M. P. Duke-ſtreet, Groſvenor-ſquare,
 London, 2 copies
David Knox, Eſq. Charlwood, Surrey
Mr William King, merchant, London
Mr. P. Kilpatrick,   do.
Mr Archibald, Knox, Sunnyſide
William Ker, Eſq. Edinburgh

L

Earl of Lauderdale
Counteſs of Lauderdale
Hon. Col. Charles Lennox, 35th regiment, 2 copies
Robert Ladbroke, Eſq. M. P. Gatton, Surrey, 2 copies
Richard Ladbroke, Eſq. Frenches do. 2 do.
Rowland Lickbarrow, Eſq. Inner Temple, London
Rev. Marmaduke Lewis, Farningham, Kent
Geo. Wenham Lewis, Weſterham, Eſq. do.
Thomas Littler, Eſq. Bernard-ſtreet, London
Thomas Latham, Eſq. London
Mrs Latham,   do.
Mr Low, Blechingly, Surrey, 4 copies
Miſs Low, Reigate, Surrey, 2 do.

Rev. John Taylor Lamb, Merftham, Surrey
Mr Love, Watling-ftreet, London
William Law, Efq. Elvingfton
Mifs Law,   do.
Mr George Leckie, merchant, London
Mr. J. Lindfay,   do.
Mrs Laurel, London
Mr Levy,   do.   2 copies
Mr Andrew Laurie, do.
Mrs Janet Little
Lieut. David Lee, Letham
Mr John Lee, Scateraw
Mr James Lee, Crawhill
Mr Charles Lorimer, Dunbar, 2 copies
Mr John Little, Edinburgh
Chriftopher Latimer, Efq.
Mr Robert Laidlaw, Finifh
Mr William Leitch

M

Duke of Montague
Vifcount Mountftuart, Hill-ftreet, London
Vifcountefs Mountftuart
Sir Jofeph Mawbey, Bart. George-ftreet, Weftminfter
Lady Mawbey
Sir William Miller, Glenlee
Hon. Mifs Murray, Elibank, 4 copies
Andrew M'Dowal, Efq. younger of Logan, M. P. 2 copies
John Maitland, Efq. younger of French
Sir William Maxwel, Monreith
Lady Ann Maitland
Right. Hon. James Montgomery, Lord Chief Baron
Mrs Montgomery, Killern
Mifs Montgomery, do.
Mifs Barbarina Montgomery, do.
James Montgomery, Efq. advocate
Capt. William Montgomery, 4th regiment foot
Patrick Murray, Efq. Simprin, 2 copies
Hon. William Maitland

Mrs Macdonald of Clanronald
Mifs Macdonald,   do.
John Macdonald, Efq. do. 2 copies
George Miller, Efq. Frankfield
James, M'Nair, Efq. Greenfield
Alexander Menzies, Efq. one of the principal Clerks of Sef-
    fion
Alexander M'Conochie, Efq. Parkhead
Allan M'Connochie, Efq. advocate, Edinburgh
William Macleod Bannatyne, Efq. do.
John Mortland, Efq.   do.
Robert Dundas M'Queen, Efq.   do. 2 copies
Mr Alexander M'Kenzie, writer to the Signet, Edinburgh
Mr Andrew M'Kenzie, do.
Mr James Marfhall, do.
Mr Thomas Manners, do.
Dr. Moore, London
Mr Muir
Duncan M'Millan, Efq. Edinburgh
George Munro, Efq. Glafgow
R. Scott Moncrief, Efq. do.
Mr Baron Mafcres, Reigate, Surrey
John Mafcres, Efq. do.
John Manfhip, Efq. India director
Mr Mann, Temple, London
Mr Alexander Maxwell, do. 4 copies
Mr William Mauduit, do. 4 do
Mr George Munro,   do.
Mifs Manderfon, Edinburgh
Rev. Matthew Murray, North Berwick
Rev. Daniel M'Queen, Prefton
Rev. Dr John Mein, Newton
Rev. John Martin, Spott
Mr James Mitchell, Haddington
Mr Charles Mitchel, writer, Edinburgh
Mr Chriftopher Middlemafs, merchant, Dunbar
Mr George Mylne, Hailes
Mr David M'Clarran, Haddington
Mr Alexander Maitland, furgeon, do.
Mr A. Miller, Glafgow
Mr Charles Milne, London,

Mr Macintoſh, London, 4 copies
Mr Mayor,   do.
Mr Molliſon,   do.
Mr Mackie,   do.
Mr Maheux,   do.
Mr Maitland,   do.
Mr Jas. Mylne, do. 2 copies
William Mackie, Eſq.
Mr Ebenezer Maſſon, merchant, Edinburgh, 3 copies
Mr William Mercer,   do.
Mr H. Mercer,   do.
Mr John Moſſman, Newcaſtle
Mr Robert Mitchell, Fiſherrow
Mr Robert Mein, Wallyford
Nicol Milne, Eſq. Fadenſide
Mr James Murray, Howden

N

Mr Niſbet, London, 4 copies
Mr Newton, do.   4 do.
Mr Thomas Nicholſon, merchant, London
Mr R. Nicholſon,   do.
Capt. George Neilſon, Queen's dragoon guards
Rev. A. Niſbet, Garvald
Mr Nevis, London
Mr Norton, Broxbourne, Hants
William Niſbet, M. D.
Mr Alexander Niſbet, merchant, Haddington
Mr Archibald, Neil, bookſeller, do.

O

Mr William Ogilvie, junior, merchant, London
Col. Oſwald, Fiſherrow
Mr Adam Ormieſton, Dunkſton

P

John Pringle, Eſq. Sheriff-depute of the county of Edin-
    burgh

Mr Poole,   London,
Mrs Prefcott,   do. 2 copies
Mr Pattle,   do.
Mrs Pattle,   do. 2 copies
Mifs Pattington,   do. 2 do.
Mr James Playfair,   do. 2 do.
Mr Samuel Philips,   do.
Mr Thomas Pinkerton, do. 4 copies
Mr John Pugh, Lamb's Conduit-ftreet, London
Mr Pigot, Mitre-court, Fleet-ftreet
Mrs Pigot, do.
——— Palmer, Efq. Richmond, Surrey
Edward Peach, Efq. Sundridge, Kent
Rev. Henry Peach, Cheam, Surrey
Mrs Paterfon, Reigate, Surrey
Mr Paterfon, do.
Mifs Paterfon, do.
Mrs Peircy, Charlotte-ftreet, Rathbone Place, London
James Peircy, Efq. Gatton, Surrey
Mrs Powel, Grove Houfe, Toating, Surrey
Rev. Thomas Pooler, rector of Gatton, Surrey
Jofeph Pickftone, Efq. Guildford
Mrs Pickftone.
Mr William Pitt, merchant, London
Mr J. O. Parr   do.
Captain Andrew Petticrew, do.
Rev. John Paton, Laffwade
Mr Andrew Pringle, junior, Balencruff-mains
Mr John Pringle, writer, Edinburgh, 2 copies
Mrs J. Peircy, Gatton, Surrey
Mr James Pringle, Haddington
Mr Thomas Pringle, do.
Mr John Pringle, Ormifton
Mr Archibald Park, Lefton
David Pearfon, Efq, Edinburgh
John Potts, Efq. Rig
Mr Alexander Palmer, Edinburgh
Mr Gideon Pott, Panchrift

c

R

Sir Richard Reynal, 2 copies
David Rae, Efq. junior of Efkgrove
William Robertfon, Efq. advocate
Adam Rolland, Efq.   do.
Mr Ruffel, London
Mrs Ruffel,   do.
Dr. Ruffel,   do.
Mrs D. Ruffel, do.
James Rennie, Efq. Leith, 2 copies
Mr John Robertfon, printer, Edinburgh
John Rigg, Efq. Mark-lane, London
John Rigg, junior, Efq.   do.
Mr Rowley, Staple Inn,   do.
Rev. James Robertfon, Ratha
Mr John Rennie, London, 4 copies
Mr John Rennie, Auldhame
Mr George Rennie, Fantacy
Mr George Robertfon writer to the fignet, Edinburgh
Mr James Robertfon   do.
John Ramfay, Efq. Ochtertyre
Dr James Robertfon
Captain Thomas Robertfon
Mr James Ruffel, Straton Mill
Mr Walter Ruffel, Pentland Mains
Rev. Neil Roy, Aberlady
Mr William Robfon, London
Mr George Ronaldfon, Marrefton
Mr Robert Roughead, Haddington
Mr John Towell Rutt, London
Mr Adam Ruffel, Brickfield
Mr Thomas Rennie, Airfield
Mr Adam Robinfon, Preftonpans
Mr James Rennie, Fallfide
Mr William Ridley, London

S

Countess of Stair
Lady Madalena Sinclair, 4 copies
Sir Robert Sinclair, Bart. of Murkle, 2 do.
Lady Sinclair, Murkle
Miss Sinclair,   do.
Honourable John Stuart, Hill-street, London
Sir James Suttie, Bart. Balgone
Robert Sinclair, Esq. advocate, 4 copies
Archibald Speirs, Esq. Elderslie
Peter Speirs, Esq. Culcreugh
James Scawen, Esq.
Miss Scawen, Betchworth, Surrey, 2 copies
Miss Louisa Scawen, Reigate, Surry
Mrs Scullard, Pendill-court, Surrey, 4 copies
William Sanxay, Esq. Epsom, Surrey
Miss Sanxay, Cheam,   do.
Miss C. Sanxay, do.   do.
Mrs Saville, Horham, Sussex
John Sharp, Esq. Gatewick, Surrey
Rev. Melmoth Skynner, Charlwood, Surrey
Rev. Joseph Sharp, Blechingly, Surrey
Mrs Scurray, Guildford, Surrey
David Sill, Esq. London
Mr Skinn, Temple, do.
Mrs Seaton, Sloane-street, London
David Smith, Esq. of Methven, advocate, Edinburgh
Mr Walter Scott, writer to the signet
Mr Moses Steven, merchant, Glasgow
Richard Somner, Esq. Haddington
Mr George Somner,   do.
Mr Richard Somner, Townhead
Mr Robert Somerville, surgeon, Haddington, 2 copies
Mr Robert Sinclair, writer to the signet
Rev. Robert Scott, Haddington
Rev. Henry Sangster, Humbie
Rev. Dr Thomas Somerville, Jedburgh
Mrs Smeton, Edinburgh

Mr John Shirreff, Mungofwells, 2 copies
Mr Patrick Shirreff, Drum, 2 do.
Mr John Shirreff, Captainhead, 2 do.
Mr David Shirreff, Dremhills 2 do.
Mr Richard Shirreff, Preston-mains
Mr James Shirreff, Edinburgh
Mr Patrick Shirreff, do.
Mr James Shirreff, London, 2 copies
Mr Alexander Shirreff, do.
Mr J. L. Shirreff, furgeon, Deptford
Mrs M. A. Shirreff, do.
Mr J. Shirreff, junior, do.
Mifs J. Shirreff, do.
Mr George Shirreff, Tyningham
Mr John Shirreff, Samuelfton
Mr David Shirreff, Kinmylies
Rev. William Smith, Muffelburgh
Mr Adam Skirvin, Garleton
Mr John Skirving, Muirton
Mr Archibald Skirving, Standingftane
Mr Robert Steel, merchant, London
Mr Robert Smithfon, do.
Mr George Spankie, merchant, Edinburgh
Mr Alexander Smith, do.
Mr Hay Smith, writer Haddington
Mr John Samuel, do.
Mr William Skirvin, Kidlaw
Mr Thomas Smith, writer, Edinburgh
Mr Robert Smith, Greenhead
Mr George Sinclair, Leith
Mr Alexander Sawyers, writer, Dunbar
Mr Charles Salter, Edinburgh
Mr John Sligo, Leith
Mr William Sligo, merchant, Leith
Mr Alexander Somerville, do.
William Stewart, Efq. Ardvorlich
Mr Charles Selkrig, accountant, Edinburgh
Walter Scott, Efq. Waughope
Adam Stavert, Efq. Hofgate
Mr Francis Sharp, merchant, Edinburgh
Mr George Spankie, do. 6 copies

Mr Matthew Shirreff, Edinburgh
Mr Archibald Simpſon, Dalkieth
Mr Walter Smith, - do.
Mr Thomas Scott, Silverbuthall
Mr Walter Scott, Preſtock
Mr William Scott, Singlo
Mr Adam Scott, Scobcleugh
Mr James Scott, Shelf-hill
Mr Charles Scott, Commonſide
Mr Francis Shiells, Edinburgh

T

Marquis of Tweedale
Marchioneſs of Tweedale
Alexander Fraſer Tytler, Eſq. Judge-Advocate
Patrick Sinclair, Threipland, Eſq. advocate, 2 copies
William Tait, Eſq.   do.
Alexander Todd, Eſq. Alderſton
Charles Henry Talbot, Eſq. Mickleham, Surrey
Mrs Talbot
Henry Turner, Eſq. London.
Coll Turner, Eſq. 4 copies
Miſs Tubb, Eaſt Grinſtead, Suſſex
George Taylor, Eſq. Carſhalton, Surrey, 2 copies
William Taylor, Eſq.
Mrs W. Taylor
Mr Patrick Thompſon, merchant, London
Mr H. Thomſon,   do.
Mr David Thomſon, writer to the ſignet
Mr John Taylor,   do.
Mr John Tait,   do.
Mr John Tait, junior, do.
Rev. John Trotter, Preſtonpans
Rev. William Torrence, Glencroſs
Mr David Tait, London, 4 copies
Mr Thomſon, do. · 2 do.
Mr Thomas Turnbull, ſurgeon, Dunbar
Henry Trotter, Eſq.
Mr Robert Tait, Preſtongrange

Mr Thomas Turnbull, Fenwick
Mr George Turnbull, Hawick
Mr John Thomson, merchant, Edinburgh

V.

Mr James Veitch, Haddington
Mr Robert Veitch, do.
Mr William Veitch, do.
Mr Robert Vernor, Fisherrow

W

The Countess Dowager Westmorland, Saville-row, London
The Earl of Wemyss, 6 copies
Sir John Wrottesley, Bart. 35th regiment
William Weymss, Esq. Cuttil-hill, 2 copies
Alexander Wight, Esq. Advocate
Mr James Walker, writer to the signet, 4 copies
John Woodford, Esq. Saville-row, London
Captain Woodford, 1st regiment, Guards
Rev. Joseph Whately, Nonsuch-park, Surrey, 4 copies
Daniel Wilson, Esq. Dallam-tower, Westmorland
Thomas Winkly, Esq. Preston, Lancashire
Mrs Winkly
Rev. Mr Whitehead, East-Grinstead, Sussex
Thomas Wakeham, Esq. do.
Mrs Wakeham
Mr Wail, Temple, London
Mr Wallington, do.
Thomas Wood, Esq. Littleton, Middlesex
Mrs Wood
Mr Wrench, Horsley, Surrey
Mr Whyte, Clapham, do.
Mr Woodrow, Wickham, Hants
Mr Wegner, Redlion-square, Wapping
—— Wallace, Esq. Carleton-hall, Northumberland
Mrs Willock, London
Miss Willock, do.

Mifs R. Willock, London
Mr Woodrow,   do. 2 copies
Mr Wright,   do.
John Wauchope, Efq. advocate
Captain James Walker, Vogric
Mr William Walker, attorney, London
Mr Francis Walker, Tanderlane
Mr Francis Walker, Whitelaw
Mr William Walker, Atholftanefoord-mains
Mr James Walker, London.
Mr George Wood, merchant, do.
Mr A. Watfon.   do.
Mr Richard Wilkinfon,   do.
Mr George Wood, furgeon,   do.
Mr George Warrock, Preftonpans
Mr William Wilfon, Paifton
Mr James White, Edinburgh
Mr John White, London
Mr William Welch, Invernefs
Mr Robert Walker, Kincardine
Mr Robert Wight, Weft Byres
Mr J. Watfon, London
Mr James Williamfon, Gorgie
Mifs Williamfon,   do.
Mr Robert Wright, Haddington
Mr William Wilfon, do.
Mr Robert Walker, Atholftanefoord
Mr Thomas Williamfon, merchant, Leith
Mr David Williamfon, Hillhead
Mr Alexander Williamfon, Fallfide
Mr James Watfon, Pinkie-mains

Y

Dr John Yule, Kendall
Mr James Yule, Fenton-barns
Mr Thomas Yates, London
Mr William Young, Edinburgh
Bailie George Young, Muffelburgh

P O E M S, ETC.

O D E

TO MR. H. D. WHEN AT THE GRAMMAR
SCHOOL OF DALKEITH.

THE ſtream of time ſtill rolling on,
 While we its current ſcarcely ſee,
In ſilence haſtes to carry down
 Whate'er is now, whate'er ſhall be.

The ſtrongeſt caſtles, higheſt tow'rs
 That waſting ſtream will level lay,
And beauty's bloom and ſpring-time's flow'rs
 As ſoon as ſeen will ſweep away.

What now the moſt important ſeems,
 Or fondly fills the youthful mind,
Shall ſoon become like laſt year's dreams,
 Which now have left no trace behind.

A

This

This friendſhip too that warms our breaſt
   Will ſoon, my HENRY, be forgot!
For how can friendſhip long exiſt
   With friends of ſuch unequal lot?

Thy birth, thy merit, may aſcend
   To higheſt honours in the ſtate!
Wilt thou remember then a friend,
   So far beneath thee plac'd by fate?

Away falſe fears that injure *him*!
   Hence low diſtruſt of *my* deſert!
If I deſerve his love, no time
   Shall wear me from my HENRY's heart!

In youth yon oak and ivy join'd;
   Not equal they! Yet cloſe they grow
Time has their boughs ſo intertwin'd,
   No force can them diſſever now.

E P I S T L E.

My Muſe, ſure, when ſhe fram'd theſe rhimes
At ſchool, dream'd of the preſent times!
At your deſire the rhimes were fram'd:
Perhaps my HENRY likewiſe dream'd,

                The

The fimile of the oak and ivy,
(Had I not been compell'd to leave thee)
Were to our cafe fo applicable,
John Gay had fpun it to a fable!
Though lefs than Gay, I mean to try it.
I'll ftick it. Well! What lofe I by it?

A FABLE.

THE OAK, THE IVY, AND THE SAGE.

IN nurfery, happy with each other,
An oak and ivy grew together,
So clofe, that all who did them fee
Thought them one individual tree.
And comelier far the tree thus feem'd,
Than either had apart been deem'd.
The ivy, green through all the year,
Did on the oak fo gay appear,
That he, before his leaves were blown,
Rejoic'd in th'ivy's as his own:
And as he rear'd his ftately top,
So high his friend was carried up,
That all the nurfery thought this ivy
Would grow a tree fit for the navy.

A 2   The

The creeping thing fo lofty rofe,
He at his betters tofs'd his nofe.
So you've feen other fav'rites do
Rais'd on fuch props above their due.

One April morning fair and mild,
All nature with the feafon fmil'd,
New flowers, new verdure cloth'd the plains,
The groves refound with new love-ftrains;
Like nature fmiling, thus the oak
To his beloved ivy fpoke:

My Ivy! thus we'll ever grow.
Thee twifted round my higheft bough,
I'll as a crown of laurel wear,
And make thee all my honours fhare.
If e'er I grow a mighty tree
My Ivy too fhall rife with me.

Alas, my Oak! the Ivy cry'd,
Fate has to me that blifs deny'd.
Had I one wifh, that wifh fhould be
To rife, to ftand, to fall with thee;
And thus th' unfading wreath to grow
Of fame, that muft adorn thy brow.
No thunder, rain, or fnow, or hail,
Should thee before thy friend affail;

No

No breeze peftiferous from the eaft,
Untimely fhould thy leaves diveft;
No rot corrupt thy nobleft part,
The true red timber of thy heart !——
But thou from beft of acorns fprung,
So ftraight fo vigorous while fo young,
Shalt foon be from thine Ivy torn,
And to the royal foreft borne ;
Where thou no axe or faw fhalt feel
Till fit to be a firft-rate keel.
Whilft I, whom forefters defpife,
Bereft of ev'ry hope to rife,
Muft, by fome trifling florift planted,
In a poor fhrub'ry, creep contented.

The planters came, while yet he fpoke,
And to the foreft bore the oak ;
Where, though he has but fhort while ftood,
You fee his top o'er all the wood.——

The Ivy, in a fhrub'ry planted,
Creeps on forgot, not difcontented :
Though once, 'tis faid, a fecret figh
Betray'd a wifh to rife more high.
A fage-bufh, that within him grew,
And all his thoughts and wifhes knew,
Beheld that wifh, though half fupprefs'd,
And in thefe words his friend addrefs'd :

Faith,

SAGE.

Faith, Mafter Ivy, I muft tell you,
You are not quite that happy fellow
Which by the world you would be thought:
Repining at your humble lot,
You often to the foreft look,
With envy on yon lofty oak.
I fee you think that were you yonder,
Like him you'd fill the world with wonder.

IVY.

Yon oak was once my friend: With him,
I own, I almoft wifh'd to climb.

SAGE.

The forefters would ne'er allow
Such hurtful weeds on him to grow.
With all your boafted ever-green,
You there had but a nuifance been.
From fuch fine trees you had been cut,
Torn down, and trampled under foot.
Climb in the foreft! Could you lick
The feet of fome old crazy ftick,
Who wants your leaves to hide fome part
That might betray his rotten heart;

His

His hollow heart where fwallows fleep,
Or pois'nous afps and adders creep.
You might mount o'er his withering top.

IVY.

What! mount on fuch a rotten prop,
Where I fhould fear at ev'ry fquall,
To fhare a corrupt patron's fall?
I would not crawl through dirt to rife,
Or join with one whom I defpife.
By vice procur'd, the higheft place,
Inftead of honour brings difgrace.

SAGE.

Not crawl through dirt? Not rife with vice?
You're for the foreft much too nice!
The foreft! No: We're better here,
Where fqualls, where tempefts bring no fear.
In th' hurricane that lately blew,
And half the foreft overthrew,
Tall oaks came thundering to the ground,
The loftieft trees all fcatter'd round;
While fafe and fhelter'd, we unhurt,
And fearlefs here laugh'd at the fport.

Ivy.

IVY.

You're right, good Sage! I muft confefs,
That here, although our pleafure's lefs,
'Tis more fecure.   No ftorms annoy,
No fears difturb our equal joy.
Here, though at no great diftance feen,
Our leaves through all the year are green.

SAGE.

Your pleafure lefs! That fcarce I grant.
What joys have they that here you want?
The winged beauties of the groves
Safe in your fhade enjoy their loves;
Among your leaves forever gay
The little minftrels fing and play:
From fummer's heat, from winter's wind,
They there a friendly fhelter find;
And there in grateful tribute bring
The earlieft mufic of the fpring.
Here fully fed in fertile ground;
You various fend your fhoots around.
While rifing o'er the garden wall,
You feem the greateft of us all.

IVY.

IVY.

This place indeed beſt ſuits our nature :
I own we could be no where better.

POET.

The ſimile's to a fable ſpun ;
So long, you thought 'twould ne'er be done!
'Twould tire you, elſe I ſtill were able
To make an Epic of my fable.
You hate long-winded allegory :
And ſo do I.——*End of the ſtory.*

Preſuming you have no objections,
I'll yet intrude——

A FEW REFLECTIONS.

The man can never hope to ſhine
That's plac'd in an improper line.
For nature his attempts would fruſtrate.
This three examples will illuſtrate.

I.

If Cicero had been our ſhaver,
He had plagu'd us with his cliſhmaclaver

B   2. Had

2.

Had Cæfar at my plough been bred,
He had broke, no doubt, his mafter's head ;
Been fent to jail—made a recruit.—
Sure th' army would his genius fuit !
He had mutiny'd—his captain bang'd,
And been, inftead of Emp'ror,—hang'd.

3.

Suppofe our places chang'd awhile :
You at this fuppofition fmile.
But, Sir, in my place, you'd been dub'd
The Prefes of an alehoufe club.
There your great fenatorial thunder
Had made knaves envy, blockheads wonder.
You had given your little fenate laws;
Your word had ended ev'ry caufe ;
For fkill in politics and tillage,
You'd been renown'd through all the village.
If you had pleas'd a book to write
You had been as great as A— W—,
But what had I done in your place ?
This ftammering tongue! this fheepifh face!
A ftatefman ! Humph ! Alas ! alas ?

A SONG.

Tune, *Woe's my heart that we shou'd sunder.*

WITH Delia's easy kindness cloy'd,
 'Twas little now that Damon priz'd her;
And whilst she at his parting cry'd,
 He with this cruel song advis'd her.
If, Delia, e'er you set your mind
 Upon a youth with mettle in him,
Seem not too ready to be kind,
 For that way you shall never win him.

No soldier boasts th' inglorious field,
 That's gain'd with little opposition:
Nor can that love a pleasure yield,
 Which gives no fuel to ambition.
We're proud to seize the swiftest game;
 We're proud to gain the richest treasure:
Ev'n love, without the hopes of fame,
 Is but a dull insipid pleasure.

'Tis

'Tis hence the haughty youth diſlikes
   The eaſy maid that fondly woes him;
And, like a ſpaniel, courts the ſtripes
   Of her that boldly dares abuſe him.
Then, Delia, juſtly prize your charms.
   When Colin courts, with caution truſt him;
And, if you'd bind him in your arms,
   Seem ſtill determin'd thence to thruſt him!

If he turn cold, affect diſdain;
   Seem careleſs, you ſhall yet enſlave him;
And drag him, in your beauty's chain,
   To marriage, or—where'er you'd have him.
Thus Damon ſung, and laughing fled.
   Delia, too late her error finding,
Wip'd her ſad eyes; and, ſighing, ſaid,
   The ſong is worth a lady's minding.

A

A SCOTS SONG.

I.

HOW pleafant ance were Lothian's plains!
　Joy fung in ev'ry cottage there!
Trig were our maidens, blyth our fwains,
　At ev'ry wedding, feaft, and fair!
Nae wedding now, nae fair, nae feaft,
　Can fill our maids or fwains wi' glee.
Care fighs in ev'ry thoughtfu' breaft,
　And fadnefs lours in ilka eye.

II.

Thefe views of Forth nae mair can pleafe;
　Now fummer fields nae mair feem gay:
Joy flies, with competence and eafe,
　Frae Lothian's groaning fwains away!
Ance winter's fharpeft froft and fnaw,
　In plenty warm, we didna fear;
But now the blafts of poortith blaw,
　Mair fharp than winter's a' the year.

III.

Now nappy ale and punch nae mair,
　At Chriftmas, fhall our fwains folace;

Where

Where vig'rous age forgot his care,
   Amidſt his childrens pratling race.
Nae ſturdy youth at bullets plies;
   Unhanded waſtes the curling-ſtane;
Uſeleſs in ſtour the golf-club lies,
   And pipers waſte their wind in vain.

IV.

Nae mair ſhall love-pair'd couples glow,
   With raptures down the rural dance;
And marks of artleſs paſſion flow
   From heart to heart, with ev'ry glance!
In joyful clubs nae mair we ſtroll,
   The garden of its ſweets to ſtrip;
Where happy Love aft ſlyly ſtole
   Far dearer ſweets frae Beauty's lip.

V.

Nae mair the ſwain by flow'ry peaſe,
   Or whitening hedge, the virgin leads.
How ſweet the fragrance of the breeze!
   Her breath that ſweetneſs far exceeds!
When laſſes wade, or waſh their claes,
   With kilted coats upon the knee,
Nae pawky ſwains keek o'er the braes
   Or cares the whiteſt legs to ſee!

VI.

VI.

And when they to the milking gang,
   Nae jokefome fhepherd brings the cow:
Alane they hum fome dreary fang;
   What fwains dow kifs or towzle now?
Dark Winter hears nae fang mair gay,
   Than *Margaret's Ghoft*, or *Foreft Flowers,*
Which in their prime were wed away
   By cruel fate——Ah! fae are ours!

VII.

Sing nae blyth fangs, yea beauteous quire!
   Each fair-wrought lad as ftiff's a rung,
Wad fa' afleep befide the fire,
   Though *John, come kifs me now* ye fung!
But ken ye whence our forrow's fpring?
   Our greedy lairds bear a' the blame.
What ance made mony a tenant fing,
   Now hardly fteghs ae landlord's wame!

VIII.

While fumptuoufly ye eat and drink,
   Does it ne'er fting your confcious breaft,
Ah, cruel luxury! to think
   He ftarves whofe toil procur'd the feaft.
Here heartlefs coofs may toil and pine,
   Some rigid tyrant's willing flaves;
But freedom fhall be ever mine?
   There's freedom yet beyond the waves!

MELPOMENE

MELPOMENE AND THALIA,

A SONG.

ADDRESSED TO DAVID GARRICK, ESQ.

MELPOMENE, a nymph divine,
   Once conquer'd with majeſtic grace;
While wiſdom gay, with wit benign,
   Charm'd in Thalia's ſmiling face.
This ſung gay notes, that plaintive ſtrains;
   Soft raptures fir'd each tender breaſt.
Ador'd they were by all our ſwains:
   But Willie far outſhone the reſt.

Sweet ſongs he ſung in both their praiſe;
   Fair flow'rs he bound on either brow:
And they crown'd him with wond'rous bays,
   Which greener as they elder grew.
Fair ſiſters! who ſhall ſing your praiſe?
   Who for your brows ſhall pick the flow'r?
Whoſe temples ſhall you crown with bays?
   Your Willie ſings, alas! no more.

Davie;

Davie, the pride of Britain's fwains,
  So charms you with the dance and fong,
That ev'n your Willie's matchlefs ftrains
  Sound fweeter now from Davie's tongue.
So well can he your garlands trim,
  So well can he adjuft your drefs,
In ev'ry point you credit him,
  Before your faithful looking-glafs.

But Davie, of your favours proud,
  Now ev'ry where his pow'r would boaft;
And, to amaze the gaping croud,
  Arrays you like each reigning toaft.
Farcia, (the lighteft of her kind,
  Who roars with drunkards thro' the town;
Who with mad fquires will chace the hind,
  Or romp about with a dragoon;)

With rough fongs makes the taverns ring;
  Davie to you thefe fongs repeats;
Like the buffoon he bids you fing,
  And rival her in monkey feats.
Thofe feats the maid of princely grace,
  With ftrangely awkward meannefs apes;
And the fweet lafs of fmiling face
  Puts on her mad diftorted fhapes.

Where

Where they appear in this difguife,:
   They raife no fweetly-tender flame;
Genius and wit their fongs defpife,
   And true tafte blufhes at their fhame;
And of this change is Davie proud?
   Ah, Davie! thou haft little caufe:
What boots it to amaze the croud,
   If Wit and Tafte refufe applaufe?

What pity, Davie! thy fweet tongue,
   Which warbles well the pureft lays,
Should be debas'd by Farcia's fong?
   Or thou be fond of Folly's praife?
Such praifes, Davie! yet defpife;
   Delude the lovely pair no more;
Let wit and tafte their beauty prize,
   Their former fame and thine reftore!

TO A LADY IN ENGLAND, WHO HAD EX-
ACTED THE AUTHOR'S PROMISE THAT HE
WOULD WRITE TO HER A WITTY LETTER.

Thae fecond-fighted folks (his peace be here!)
See things far aff, and things to come, as clear
As I can fee my thumb.———
GENTLE SHEPHERD.

DEAR KITTY,

OF Scotfmen's fecond-fight you'll find,
   In Johnfon's Tour, fine ftories:
Whate'er will much affect our mind,
   Though diftant, feems before us.
To prove the Doctor tells you true,
   Though Englifhmen may wonder,
I'll let you know I talk with you
   Four hundred miles afunder.

I heard you fay to your aunt laft night;
   (Say, Michael, did'nt you hear it?)
" Friend Mylne is lazy fure to write!
   " How thinks he I fhould bear it?
C 2 " He

" He promis'd me, a year agone,
  " Some witty lines and clever.
" He promis'd much! Ay so does one
  "'Who means to pay us never.

" Shall we have clever Englifh rhimes
  " From that poor fide of Tweed,
" Where hungry bards in frozen climes
  " Can fcarce our language read?
" Thinks he poor Scotland's alloy'd brafs
  " Would pafs with us for better?
"' I'll have my debt in fterling cafh;
  " Or hold him ftill my debtor."

Four hundred miles this dunning found
  I heard, with fpirits finking:
Fatal as Shylock's was the bond,
  Which I fubfcrib'd unthinking.
The bond's unpaid: The forfeit due:
  For witlefs is my fonnet.
Should Kitty, cruel as the Jew,
  Infift with rigour on it;

I've only poor Anthonio's way:
  Since I like him am bound,
And have no wit wherewith to pay,
  Take of my heart a pound.

                *   *   *   *

                        DESOLATION,

DESOLATION,

A PASTORAL.

COLIN, ASPER, AND MENALCAS.

COLIN.

'TWERE better, Asper, to continue here;
Like me, be frugal, if your farm be dear;
Late end your toil, and early rise to work.

ASPER.

I'll rather bear a musket for the Turk!
All other slaves get food from those they serve:
For cruel masters farmers toil, and starve!

COLIN.

You yet may get a tolerable lease!

ASPER.

Where is the landlord now that gives us these?

COLIN.

COLIN.

Still there are such!

ASPER.

In Scotland?

COLIN.

Two or three
Take pleafure yet a thriving fwain to fee,
In their dependent's happinefs rejoice,
And help induftrious honefty to rife.

ASPER.

Are their old tenants never turn'd away,
Helplefs in age and indigence to ftray?

COLIN.

No! If mifchance their fwains to hardfhips drive,
They eafe his wants, and help him ftill to thrive.

ASPER.

Then they, fome future fhepherd's grateful
　　　theme,
Shall live with *Cockburn* in immortal fame:
While thefe proud Squires, who now feem
　　　men of note,
Shall, with the deer they've fwallow'd, lie forgot.

COLIN.

COLIN.

With our good landlords, no projectors vain,
Servants grown rich, or merchants crack'd in
     brain,
Promising rents the lands can never yield,
E'er turn'd a worthy farmer from his field.

ASPER.

But Satan offering here one penny more,
Would turn ev'n Cincinnatus to the door.

COLIN.

For this the tenants have themselves to blame:
When honest Thirsis broke, in crouds they came,
And strove with ardour who should offer most
For that poor farm, where all his stock was lost.

ASPER.

Yes, Thirsis broke: but they are men of parts,
And to work wonders have ten thousand arts!

COLIN.

Our Squire soon found the greatest coxcomb
     out,
And little flatt'ry brought his end about:
                            Aye!

" Aye! you have parts indeed! you underftand
" Alone the value of fuch fertile land!
" Upon my honóur, you're a lad of life,
" And fuch a perfon for a rich young wife!"
But fimple gull! does he your brothers tear?
Does he devour a tenant ev'ry year?
And will you then the very dangers run,
That fuch examples call to you to fhun?

ASPER.

Examples they behold not! Mangled flies
Mark the foul corner where the fpider lies:
But does their fate make other flies beware?
Still numbers, thoughtlefs, buzz into the fnare.
Proceed, ye Squires! fqueeze with unfparing
        hand!
You'll ftill find fools to give too much for land!

COLIN.

But thofe will break, and then their rents will
        fall.

ASPER.

No!—Other fools will give them ftill their all.
Go live at court, a prey to fharpers there!
When others fpeak, in wife-like filence ftare!
                                        Or;

Or, sleeping at a parliament debate,
Dream of rich posts, and favours of the great:
While all your ill your depute here exceeds,
And makes your name excuse his harshest deeds!
He writes you, how your rents increase at home:
Increase th' expence! think not of times to come!,
When rags and vermine are your tenants stock,
Your villages all theft, filth, stink, and smoke!
When howling misery your house surrounds,
And desolation marks your horrid bounds!
Your vassal-slaves go one by one to pot!
In all your land you cannot raise a groat!
Go, put your tenants tatter'd rags to sale!
Your land must fly to keep you out of jail!

COLIN.

Our parson says, Where superstition reigns,
Where priestly rigour squeezes Roman swains,
Desert and waste the groaning land appears,
And ev'ry face distress's features wears.
In vain has nature giv'n a fertile soil:
Each prudent swain flies from the fruitless toil.
Ah! shall our land to such a state decay?
Yes! all her worthiest sons are torn away!
None who seek wealth can hope to find it here;
All who love ease to foreign climates steer:

D   The

The generous follow freedom o'er the waves!

ASPER.

None stay but wretches willing to be slaves!

COLIN.

Through twenty future years methinks I see
The plight in which our country then shall be!
How sadly droops each late-repenting swain,
Whose folly bound him to a life of pain!
Sore whip'd, his lean, old horses, groaning go;
Nor whistles th' hungry driver of the plough!
The master at the fruitless labour sighs,
And wipes the secret sorrow from his eyes.
While in her dark and dirty house forlorn,
Bare to the bone with care and hunger worn,
On the cold hearth that seldom feels a flame,
Hard at her household labour plies the dame.
But wretched mother! who shall speak thy pain,
When naked children cry for bread in vain!

ASPER.

Let ev'ry honest swain forsake this shore,
Where easy freedom lives with swains no more.
Behold yon lawyer! fly his harpy hand!
What numbers starve on his late-purchas'd land!

Long

Long has he practis'd ev'ry art to fqueeze,
And hoards, with fordid care, his double fees!
From plea to plea his clients are led on,
Till credit fails, and then th' account is fhown?
In every line it feems a moderate charge!
But at the foot—Good heav'ns—a fum fo large!
Why, Sir, it doubles all that I poffefs!
" No lawyer in the town would do't for lefs!
" We've long been friends; with you I will
          " not ftand;
" I'll take no more from you, but—all your
          " land!"

Wide fpreads his land! his undiftinguifh'd prey,
Tenants and fquires, he feafts on ev'ry day.
Thorns yield no grapes!—But, men of rank,
          will you
A fhamelefs pettifogger's fteps purfue?
If you would ftill have men your rank revere;
If by your *honour* ftill you wifh to fwear;
Defend it now!—Warm with true honour,
          hafte
To ftem this tide that lays your country wafte.

COLIN.

Refign'd to ruin amongft wither'd trees,
See many an antient dome; in each of thefe
                                        Once

Once liv'd fome worthy lord, or knight, or
  fquire!
The poor and ftranger nightly bleft his fire!
He liv'd at home, and fpent his income there;
Mechanics, merchants, farmers, had their fhare.
His wealth fpread happinefs o'er all the plain,
Soon went its round, and came to him again:
Then well-paid induftry with pleafure toil'd,
And all around the populous country fmil'd.

ASPER.

A tyrant harpy now has bought them all,
Racks high the rents, but lets the manfions fall.

COLIN.

From this next ruin, Afper, here behold
A piteous fight! Menalcas weak and old!
Who, with pale famine ftaring in his face,
Laments the change of that once happy place!

MENALCAS.

Alas! my neighbours! how my heart is rent,
To fee thefe walls where my beft days were
  fpent,
Thus overgrown with hemlock, grafs, and mofs!
As well as mine it fpeaks the country's lofs!
        Here

Here once the voice of happy pleafure fung,
With mirth's loud laughter diftant echoes rung.
In ale and mufic funk the night. The morn
Was waken'd by the chearful hound and horn.
Happy himfelf, my Lord rejoic'd to fee
Each face around reflect his inward glee!
Now deadly filence ever round it fleeps,
Unlefs when here my fad remembrance weeps.
Ah! wafting walls! your laft remaining tower
Shakes in each blaft, and melts in ev'ry fhower!

COLIN.

Upon its rotten roof hangs but one flate?—

MENALCAS.

But painted ceilings fpeak its former ftate!
Though daws and fwallows lodge their filthy
    young,
Where pictures of the family's worthies hung;
Rats, frogs, and toads, the fpacious halls defile,
Where gayeft beauties wont of old to fmile.
Where once fweet minftrels charm'd the dan-
    cing throng,
Th' ill-boding owl now howls the whole night
    long.

Sad,

Sad, through the parlour, nightly fighs the
      ghoft
Of him who once fat there the jovial hoft:
Sees in his vaults, where ripening hogfheads
      ftood,
Badgers and foxes rear their ftinking brood.
Docks, hemlocks, nettles, overgrow the court,
Where oft his youthful tenants us'd to fport.
There many a feat of ftrength and fkill were
      fhown;
The Chief was judge, nor fcorn'd to fhow his
      own.
When young, he often carried off the bays;
When old, he prais'd his ftrength in former
      days:
To yon high mark, in youth he heav'd the
      ball;
His ftronger father tofs'd it o'er the wall.
Then each, invited, was a welcome gueft;
And next the Baron was the victor plac'd.

ASPER.

Such happinefs our fathers faw,—but we
Muft feek our food beyond th' Atlantic fea;
                  Where

Where true-born children of this boasting isle
Already at their mother's mandates smile;
Loll out their tongue at honest father Bull,
Despise his rod, and all his acts annul,
Trust not, ye tyrants, to those children's
    love
Whom your harsh rigours from your confines
    drove
Brave Martius' patriot flames were turn'd to
    hate;
And Rome, from him she banish'd, fear'd
    her fate!
Your few sad slaves will trembling die with
    fear,
When of th' invading colonies they hear;
Or gladly run to welcome us ashore,
When the delivering thunders round you
    roar.
The wind is up! The ship is under sail!
My native land, be d——d.——My friends,
    farewell.

TO MR. BURNS,

ON HIS POEMS.

ON yon green fod what maiden fits,
  Wi' garland dow'd, and looks forlorn!—
Lord keep the laffie in her wits!
  She fings, and yet fhe feems to mourn!
Do ye no ken the Scottifh mufe?
  Here aft fhe feeks her darling fhade:
And aft wi' tears that grave bedews,
  Where poor *Rob Fergufon* was laid.

But whifht! fhe fpeaks?—" My deareft callan,
  " A fair ftroke was thy death to me!
" For, fince I loft my winfome *Allan*,
  " My only hope was fheught in thee?
" Nae mair our verfes, fmooth and ftrang,
  " Our men to martial fame incite:
" Or warbled in melodious fang,
  " Our maidens melt wi' faft delight.
                                " Our

" Our language, banifh'd now frae court,
  " (For Scotland has nae court at hame)
" Is lightly'd by the better fort;
  " And ilka coof maun mimic them.
" New-fangled fools gade to the South,
  "And brought frae court new fafhion'd frazes,
" That gar our auld anes found uncouth;
  " And ev'n our mother's words bombaze us.

" Affected foplings feinzie fhame
  " Of ilka thing benorth the Tweed:
" But wha wad fafh their head wi' them!
  " The blockheads fcarce a word can read."
" Ged tak me, Mam, I kennot read
  " Thees your owld-fafhion'd vulgar Scotch!"
" Half Scots, half Englifh, they proceed,
  "Smafhing baith tongues to bafe hotch potch.

" We flatter thus a friend, when braw,
  " And cringe to him when gear is fent him;
" But when his back is at the wa',
  " We blufh to own that e'er we kent him.
" I little thought ance in a day,
  " When our ain bards fae fwcetly fung,
" That gloffaries we boot to hae,
  " To teach Scots men their native tongue.

E   " Or

" Or that our fangs, fae peerlefs good,
  "Thro'this falfe tafte, this pride new-fangled,
" Boot be, to mak them underftood,
  " In *Englifh verfions* *, vilely mangled.
" Afore he wrote, bauld *Ramfay* faw
  " The fmeddom o' our tongue decay ;
" His words, as if caukt on a wa',
  " Were wearing fainter ilka day.

" Yet he in nature's genuine ftrains
  " Our feelings fae diftinctly draws,
" He'll ever on his native plains,
  " And foreign too, command applaufe.
" Our dying tongue, by him reviv'd,
  " At *Allan*'s death again grew faint :
" Till thou, my *Fergufon !* arriv'd,
  " And feem'd frae heav'n ance errant fent,

" To teach the warld that fimple lays,
  " In nature's language, reach the heart ;
" And frae true genius get the praife
  " Deny'd to ftiff refining art.—
" But *Robin*'s fp'rit at laft is here,
  " Wi' pleafure fmiling on his brow !—
                                  " Whare

* See Ward's Gentle Shepherd.

" Whare ha' ye been, gin ane may fpeer ?
　" And what maks ye fae blyth, my dow ?"

" When wand'ring between Ayr and Doon,
　" I faw a laddie at the pleugh:
" But Mufe ! a fang I heard him crune,
　" That ftill feems in my lugs to fough."

" Fallow mortal ! why fae haftie ;
" Banifh terror frae thy breaftie ;
" Wae's me for the chance that chac'd thee
　　　" Frae thy fnug houfie."
" 'Twas fome way that way ; and addreft to
　　　" A till'd-up moufie.

" He loos'd his pleugh. I rade wi' him
　" On his auld white mare, fonfie Maggie ;
" Wha, proud to think fhe'd live in rhime,
　" Cockt head and tail, like ony ftaiggie.
" I lookt into his breaft, and faw
　" Compaffion for his fallow-creature,
" Amang the feelings, ane and a',
　" That maift embellifh human nature.

" I looked up into his head——
　" Gude lofh !—What bright poetic fancies !
　　　" A'

" A' ſtriving whilk ſhou'd hae the lead,
  " In ſooh-intended rhiming dances.
" True judgement there directed a',
  " And let them out in proper order ;
" Imagination buſkt them braw ;
  " And memory ſat clark-recorder.

" The virtues a' to recommend
  " Meetly appear'd their common aim ;
" But their true motive (weel I kend)
  " Was ardour for poetic fame.
" I ſaw them plan, in calked lines,
  " Some ſleely-jibing admonitions,
" To drive our dour, dull Scots divines
  " Frae gloomy, canting ſuperſtitions.

" I ſaw them plan the *Cottar's ingle* ;
  " Where happy ſat man, wife, laſs, callan :
" And, in the general joy to mingle,
  " Ev'n hawkie routs ayont the hallan.
" Frae hawkie comes the haleſome feaſt,
  " On which well-pleas'd they ſup or dine ;
" And in thae ſober draughts maiſt bleſt,
  " They never think of coſtly wine.

" Cracks, tales, and ſangs, them canty keep,
  " Till th' hours bring wonted bed-time roun';
                          " Then

" Then found on caff or ftrae they fleep,
" While gentles, fleeplefs, fret on down.
" Blufh, Greatnefs, at your ill-fpent time!
" To you fuch blifs is feldom given.
" Can ye conceive the thoughts fublime,
" On which they rife frae earth to heaven?

" Ablins the while your groveling thoughts
" Are fome infernal purpofe brewing,
" To turn them frae their peacefu' cotts,
" Or a' their peace, and *Jenny*, ruin *.
" Thae fancies, when they wad befriend
" The poor folk, flow in faft fucceffion ;
" And when harfh mafters they wad bend,
" Their very tykes bark at oppreffion.

" They'll fing in hamely paftoral ftile,
" (For which nae nation e'er cou'd brag us),
" Sangs that will aye gar Scotland fmile
" At whifky, or a good fat haggies.
" In foothing, fympathifing ftrain,
" They fhall revive the heart that mourns."
" Then cried the Mufe, a' fidging fain,
" I fee you've found my *Robbie Burns!*

" He

---

* An allufion to Burns's poem of the Cottar's Saturday night.

" He frae his birth has been my care!
  " He, till he dies fhall be the.fame;
" And fangs frae him ye'll fhortly hear,
  " To rival yours, and *Ramfay*'s fame."

Then crew the cock.   The vifion fled.
And whare was I?—Juft in my bed!
The dream ay fiftling in my head,
        I cou'd na 'reft;
But to write this to *Burns*, I faid,
        I'll do my beft.

My beft!—Alake!—Write *Burns!*—O fy!
What is there *Burns* can ken me by?
Though fometimes in the Mufe's pye
        I've had a finger,
I've only fhown, I fear, that I
        Am nae great finger.

For had the few lines I hae penn'd
Been worth, they had been better kenn'd.
Confcious myfel they'd thole amend,
        I ne'er durft print them;
But wore them in my pouch t'an end,
        Or brunt or tint them.

                    Yet

Yet I commend your nobler daring,
That, fpite of critics and their jarring,
Cou'd bring to light your lines auld-farran,
   That mak fic din ;
And they've brought gowd to you I'fe warran,
   In gowpens in.

I ken ye dinna care a fnuff
For a' the filly fleeching ftuff,
Wi' which the like o' me now puff
   Ye in prefumption ;
For, though few bards be flattery-proof,
   Ye've rummle-gumption.

But Lord man! tell me, how is't wie ye,
When ilka great man that ye fee
Hads out his hand, or jouks to thee?
   Are n' ye fae fain
Ye're like to fwelt?—I'm fure wer't me,
   'Twad turn my brain!

Yes, cock (as weel ye may) your creft,
And prize the praifes o' the beft !
But tent this :—Feather now your neft.
   Hain for a fair foot.
Syne ye may dine, when fome o' the reft
   Maun lick the hare foot.

       Ramfay

Ramsay at firſt, an' 'twas his due,
Was courted, prais'd, careſt, like you :
That ſangs and poets pleaſe maiſt when new,
   He wiſely kend ;
And ſtill made ſangs, an' jeeſies too,
   And ſiller hain'd.

Forgot, when auld, (I mind myſell)
He liv'd upon the Caſtle-hill,
Scarce ane e'er ſpeer'd whare he did dwell,
   Or aught about him.
But what car'd *Allan*? He cou'd bell
   The cat without them.

Sae prudence bids you buſineſs chuſe,
And no truſt a' thing to the muſe.
O'er aft we've ſeen the jilt miſuſe
   The beſt o' poets ;
And mak them fain to pawn their hoſe,
   For ſlip-ſlap diets.

Soon as his friends wi' praiſe inflame
The youthfu' bard to flee at fame,
Quite ſpoilt for ilka ither game,
   His thoughts tak flight,
And leave his cares, affairs, and hame,
   Clean out o' ſight.

        The

'The gowd of a' thae parts far eaft,
Whare fpite of fame, health, confcience, reft,
E'en ne'er-do-wells foon fill their kift,
    Affects him little:
In poetry he to ding the beft,
    Plys a' his mettle.

The live-lang day his fangs he'll crune,
To th' burnie or the breeze's tune;
But finds, when near life's afternoon,
    He's a' wud wrang:
His fhoon, hofe, fark, breeks, a' thing done,.
    Except his fang.——

It fets me weel to gie advice!
Have I myfell been aye fae wife?
My game, when I threw lucky dice,
    Have I ne'er fticket?
What have I made my words to fplice?
    Made?—Deil be licket.

I've feen fome wha begoud wi' lefs,
On whafe head few lay muckle ftrefs,
Wi' fheep and runts ftock, blads o' grafs;
    While I hae nathing,
      F   But

But meat, drink, health, content, and peace,
   And fire and claithing.

The wyte, when I lay on the mufe,
She tells me aye, herfel t'excufe,
That I was ne'er fae gair as thofe
    Wham wit ca's dull.
Ye'll fee, quo' fhe, fpite o' your nofe,
    Wha's been maift fool.

I hope ye think na to befpatter ye,
Like mony mae wi' fulfome flattery,
Far lefs to roufe your anger's battery,
    Was my intent.
To let ye ken I'd like to clatter wi' ye,
    Was a' I meant.

I feldom cringe to wealth or fame,
Or o' their friendfhip count the name:
For the maift feck I live at hame,
    A farmer douce,
Amang my bairnies and their dame,
    In this thackt houfe.

        Whare

Whare we'd be glad to fee ye, Gabbie!
Fine fare I winna hecht.   How n' a' be,
Although we fhou'd hae but ae fybie,
          Ye'fe get your fkair.
We'll aye get fa't to it ; and may be,
          Can barrow mair.

I downa bide to hear a glutton
Fraifing about fine beef and mutton;
I never ken or care a button
          What I'm to get ;
But leave the wife her will to put on
          The pat or fpit.

The hoft diflikt, nae fumptuous fare,
Nae ven'fon, turtle, or fic ware,
Wi' wines maift coftly, rich, and rare,
          Which bring fome guefts,
Shou'd e'er mak me green to come near
          Him or his feafts.

My mind in this ye partly fee.—
Gif ye diflike it, let it be.—
But gif it chance to pleafe, and ye
          Think it worth while,

         Eaftward

Eaſtward frae Edinbrugh by the ſea,
   But fourteen mile;

Ride through the town o' Preſtonpans;
Three miles ayont that leave the ſands;
Then ither twa thro' gude rich lands,
   You'll find Loch-hill,
And, ready to rin at your commands,
   Your friend
      JAMES MYLNE.

CHORUS,

C H O R U S,

IN THE ANCIENT MANNER.

On-the death of the celebrated *Cuchullin*, who was guardian to *Cormac* the infant monarch of Ireland, and who ruled the kingdom in his minority, *Cairbar*, Lord of Atha, at the head of a great band of rebels, befieged the royal palace of *Temora*; and having barbaroufly put to death the young *Cormac*, together with the fons of fome of the chief nobility, ufurped the government of the kingdom. *Fingal*, fovereign of Caledonia, being early apprized of the rebellion of *Cairbar*, had fent his grandfon *Ofcar* with fome troops to the affiftance of *Cormac*. In the interval, and before intelligence arrived of the melancholy fate of the young monarch, the fcene, which is the fubjeƈt of the following Chorus, is fuppofed to pafs in the royal hall of *Selma*, where *Fingal* is fitting in the midft of his nobles, together with his fon *Offian*, and the attendant bards.

SCENE,

SCENE,—*Fingal's hall in Selma.*

FINGAL, OSSIAN, NOBLES, LADIES, BARDS
ATTENDING.

A difmal found is heard of diftant fhrieking.

FIRST BARD,

WHAT fhrieks!

SECOND BARD,

What hideous groans!

FINGAL.

I know too well!

FIRST BARD.

Some dire prefage!

SECOND BARD.

Some grief is nigh!

FINGAL.

FINGAL.

Some fpirits thus are wont to tell
When thofe moft dear to Fingal die,

FIRST BARD.

Felt ye that blaft?
How fwift it pafs'd!

SECOND BARD.

Methought it fhook the hall!

THIRD BARD.

What meteors there!
What lightnings blaze!

FIRST BARD.

Oh!—thefe portend
A king, or kingdom's fall!

OSSIAN.

Every breath new horror brings!
Hark, hark, my harp! no human hand
    Has touch'd the ftrings!

That

That found fo difmal, hollow, low,
Foretells approaching news of woe!

FINGAL.

Strike, Offian! ftrike thy harp, my fon!
Call out the deep-refounding, folemn tone:
Sing on, till fome compaffionating ghoft
Come to tell what friends we've loft!

OSSIAN.

Spirits of our fathers dead!
    Whether ye glide
Smoothly o'er the cryftal waves;
Whether in the whirlwind's blaft,
    Ye roll the whitening tide;
Or pour the night-fhriek on the lonely hill;
    Or murmur o'er your graves!
Come in your cloudy cars,
    And tell in founds of woe,
For what departed chiefs
    Muft our deep forrows flow!

CHORUS.

For what departed chiefs, &c.

OSSIAN.

OSSIAN.

Tell me of Ofcar, tell,
  Who fails the ftormy main:
Oh! have you feen my darling fon
  Amid his martial train?

Say, does brave Ofcar live;
  Or are his fhips difpers'd,
And he, with all his band,
  In wat'ry tombs immers'd?

Or, have they reach'd green Ullin's fhores,
  And yet have come too late
To fave the fons of Ufnoth brave,
  And Cormac, from their fate?

CHORUS.

Spirits of our fathers dead!
  Let us blind mortals know
For what departed chiefs
  Muft our deep forrows flow!

G   BARD

BARD OF THE SECOND SIGHT.

Invoke no ghofts to tell you this!
Blindnefs, mortals, here is blifs!
I fee, I fee, with inward light,
I fee, and curfe the dire anticipated fight
Which brings too foon my pain.
I fee, I fee, beyond the deep
A fcene that fhall make thoufands weep!

CHORUS FIRST.

What fcene?

CHORUS SECOND.

What fcene?

CHORUS THIRD.

What fcene?

BARD.

Ye hear the fhrieks! I fee the ghofts!
Trembling they come from Erin's coafts,
Deterr'd by bloody horrors thence!

CHORUS

CHORUS FIRST.

What blood? What horror? Tell the worſt!

CHORUS SECOND.

Speak, ſpeak!

CHORUS THIRD.

Oh ſpeak, we're all ſuſpence!

BARD.

Oſcar is ſafe! He holds his way!
Tight are his ſhips, his warriors gay!
They ſoon ſhall land—and yet too late!
The ſons of Uſnoth too are well!
The reſt, the reſt, oh urge me not to tell!

CHORUS.

Oh! tell the worſt of Fate!

BARD.

Oh horror! murder! ſight of woe!

G 2

CHORUS.

CHORUS.

Tell, oh tell us, all you know!

BARD.

Look not now on Ullin's fhore!
　　See ye not the ftreaming gore?
　　Erin's young nobles now no more
　　Shall Erin's expectations raife!——
　　Cormac and his youthful peers
　　Sporting with their fathers fpears
　　Practife the feats of riper years!
Their little bofoms feel the warrior's flame!
Their little bofoms feaft on future fame!
　　But death's dark night the whole deftroys!

CHORUS.

Death's dark night the whole deftroys?

BARD.

Cairbar! Atha's gloomy Lord,
Wherefore doft thou draw the fword?
Murderer! Coward! They are boys!

CHORUS.

CHORUS.

Is there no hand to fave? no fword
To ftrike the murderers and prevent the blow?

BARD.

There is no hand to fave, or fword!
  Ghofts that glut in human gore
  Grimly glooming, ftalk before!
  Murder grins at every door!
    Fly? They cannot fly!
In heaps they fall!—they die!—they fall,
  Murder'd in Temora's hall!
  Erin's youthful nobles, all
    Around poor Cormac lie!

CHORUS.

  Murder'd in Temora's hall
    With murder'd Cormac die?

BARD.

Cormac lives yet!—The fword is rais'd!
  What gallant youth art thou

That

That intercept'ft the falling edge ?—
  Oh moft unworthy blow !

Though generoufly, though nobly done,
  Thou giv'ft thy king but fhort relief !
  Oh heart-confounding grief !
'Tis Colla's fon !——

CHORUS.

————————His only fon ?

BARD.

With his lov'd Prince he leaves the light !
He dies ! his morning fun is fet in endlefs
      night !

CHORUS.

Cormac and Colla's only fon !
Alas ! their days were fcarce begun !

BARD.

The murd'rous fcene—is done!

CHORUS.

CHORUS.

What wonder that afflicted ghosts
Fly from thefe unhappy coafts?
What wonder that all nature mourn'd;
   That harps fpontaneous moan;
That diftant hills felt and return'd
   Their dying groan!
A deed fo horrible, fo foul, was never told
By modern Seer, or bard of old!

FINGAL.

In fweetly-foothing, melancholy ftrains
   Sing, Offian, to their gentle fpirits fing!
Allay the anguifh of their dying pains!
   Let them with joy to their new manfions
      fpring!

OSSIAN.

Defcend to greet them, friendly fhades
   Of kindred gone before!
Conduct them, wond'ring and afraid,
   The regions new t' explore!

Rife,

Rife, gentle, ftranger-fpirits, rife!
　　Pain ye no more fhall know;
In leaving life's uncertain joys,
　　Ye leave its certain woe!

Ye cannot fee, indeed your names
　　Among the great inroll'd;
But thorny are the paths to fame;
　　And few are blefs'd when old!

Your fathers bleeding hearts, alas!
　　Which fondly once conceiv'd
The hopes that you fhould fill their place,·
　　Are of all hopes bereav'd!

But had they died, like you when young,
　　They now had foundly flept,
They had not flourifh'd in the fong—
　　Nor for their children wept!

CHORUS.

Spirits of Erin! ceafe to mourn!
　　Too late ye our affiftance feek!
Home to your airy dwellings turn;
　　No more on Morven's mountains fhriek!

FINGAL.

FINGAL.

Call in the wreftlers from the green,
 The nimble hunters from the heath!
Shall we in idle fports be feen?
 No—Let us hafte t'avenge their death!

CHORUS.

Spirits of Erin fpeed the happy gales!
 Strengthen each fav'ring current and each
 wave!
Fly fwiftly homeward on our fwelling fails!
 Hafte to avenge the dead, and the furvi-
 vors fave!

H FRAGMENT

FRAGMENT

OF ANOTHER CHORUS.

SCENE,—*The fea-fhore. The army landing by
Moon-light.*

BARDS AND SOLDIERS.

FIRST BARD.

GLIDE on, fair, fplendid Queen of Night,
  Through yon ferene and fable fky !
White-fkirted clouds blaze all with light !
  Darknefs beyond the mountains fly !
     Ye winds your breath reftrain !
     Thou palely-fhining main
     Still all thy fwelling waves !
Ye ghofts, who with malicious joy
Mifguided mariners annoy,
     Reft in your hollow caves !

                      Come

Come fathers, brothers, children, whom
  We loft, when lately here before.
Your fame we fung! We rais'd your tomb!
  The lofs of you we ftill deplore!
With good-portending omens come,
  And welcome us afhore!

SOLDIER.

Glimm'ring in the moon's pale light,
  Yonder ftones of difmal white,
    Mournful, mark the places where,
      With many a tear,
      Our friends we laid.
    Some of us too muft lie there!
But be not thence difmay'd.
In *Swaran's* wars though many fell,
Yet many more were left to tell
  How they with honour fought;
And how they fell as foldiers ought.
      Inevitable fate
      Awaits us all:
But come it foon, or come it late,
  Like them renown'd we'll fall!
        *   *   *   *   *

A

A LYRIC DIALOGUE

BETWEEN A

BEAU AND A SOLDIER.

BEAU.

HE plays a foolish game
Who hazards life for fame,
And on that fame relies
T' infpire love's flame.
For fhould the lofs of limbs or eyes
His ftrength or beauty maim,
The ladies would the fool defpife,
With all his boafted fame.
Ha! what avails, that in the bloody field
The foldier has made thoufands yield,
See by fome gayer youth, in love more fkill'd,
The hero's miftrefs from him torn!
How foldier, how fhall this be borne?
Better with fteel had thou been kill'd
Than with a woman's fcorn!

SOLDIER.

SOLDIER.

Away filly fopling ! How vainly ye rave !
  To think that fuch dunces as you,
Will e'er by the fair be efteem'd like the
      brave,
  With victory's wreaths on his brow !
      Such painted moth-flies
      The ladies defpife;
      Though rolling your eyes,
      Though heaving foft fighs,
Ye think ye are wonderous charming !
Though fmiling moft fweetly, though look-
    ing fo wife ;
Though frifking and lifping out ignorant
    lies,
The conduct of foldiers ye dare criticife,
  And of battles and fieges determine !
A foldier who wants both his limbs and his
    eyes
  Is worth twenty tribes of fuch vermine.

THE

BRITISH KINGS,

A

TRAGEDY.

PERSONS.

CADWALLAN, King of the *Britons.*
OSRICK, King of *Northumbria.*
KENWAL, King of *Weſſex.*
OSWALD, Son of *Kenwal.*
ANFRID, the Friend of *Oſrick.*
ARTHUR, a Prince of the *Britons.*
BRUDUS, the friend of *Cadwallan.*
An old Druid.

LADIES.

EMMA, *Cadwallan's* Queen.
LENA, *Oſrick's* Queen.
ELFRIDA, Daughter of *Kenwal.*
ETHA, Friend of *Emma.*
HANNA, attending *Elfrida.*

Officers, Soldiers, &c.

ACT I. SCENE I.

A WOOD.

Enter haſtily Lena and Elfrida.

LENA.

ONWARD yet farther!—Let me not again
Be dragg'd by ruffians! O my generous Prin-
    ceſs!
But lead me by the wildeſt, pathleſs groves,
Into the center of this foreſt's darkneſs;
Then leave me!—Solitude beſt ſuits me now.

ELFRIDA.

Here, where the woods firſt cover us, and we,
Unſeen ourſelves, ſee all the adjacent plain,
I told my maid, that we would wait her
    coming.
She brings with her two ſuits of mens attire,

Which I provided; left in thefe rude times
Of war and danger, if unfortunate,
It might feem fafeft to conceal our fex.
So garb'd, like youthful warriors, will we
      find
My father's camp. We in an hour may reach
That fanctuary, the moft fecure for you.

LENA.

O let me rather find among thefe wilds
Some cavern in the earth or clifted rock;
Where I may lay me down, and weep away
My few remaining hours of mifery.

ELFRIDA.

What mean thy words? Wouldft thou re-
      linquifh fo
The hopes that beauty, youth, and fortune
      give thee
Of many years of future happinefs?

LENA.

My happy years are gone! My confcious
    foul

                        Thinks

Thinks all who look on me have known my
      fhame;
And look but to infult my abject ftate!

ELFRIDA.

Let fear of infult, let remorfe and fhame,
With all their tortures tear Cadwallan's heart!
That harden'd heart!—Good heav'ns! Can
      fuch men be?
Difgrace of human nature! Such there are
Who find a fiend's enjoyment in the wreck
And forrow which they bring on ruin'd vir-
      tue!
But though with loathing and averfion thou
Haft borne fuch injury from brutal violence,
None will infult thee. Why fhould thy pure
      breaft
Feel any pangs like thofe the guilty feel?

LENA.

What fharper pangs can the moft guilty
      feel?
My fpirit all-indignant, now detefts
Thefe its polluted limbs, and longs to leave
      them.

ELFRIDA.

Now none remains of Edwin's race, but
    you,
To fill Northumbria's throne, with valiant
    Ofrick,
The worthy husband of your youthful choice.
Think, if you now without descendants die,
He must resign that kingdom to another.

LENA.

I ne'er can see him more!

ELFRIDA.

        Not see thy Lord?
Thou loved'st him sure?

LENA.

        Lov'd him! Where was that wealth,
That power, or titles that could make me
    wed,
Through avarice or ambition, where I lov'd
    not!

                His

His race unknown, no wealth or friends had
    he !——
His merit won, and ftill retains my heart !

ELFRIDA.

But was the fecret of his birth ne'er known?

LENA.

That oft we fought, but ne'er could yet
    unravel.
A paper, found among his infant-weeds,
Declar'd him nobly born : To that great truth,
His form majeftic, his exalted mind,
Unfolding with his years, gave ampleft proof,
And forc'd affent.   His every action now,
Ranks him among the firft of Albion's heroes.
Love him ?—Alas !——But fhall 1 make him
    wretched ?

ELFRIDA.

Moft wretched would the lofs of Lena
    make him.

LENA.

LENA,

More wretched would he be to fee her thus
Polluted!——In fome unfrequented grove
With filent anguifh will I caft me down,
Determin'd never more to rife to light.
The ghoft, perhaps, of one who there has
    fallen,
Like me, the victim of defpair, unfeen,
Shall figh with me in fympathetic founds:
Or filently according with my foul,
Raife from the earth its fentiments, attun'd
To the full harmony of heavenly thought.

ELFRIDA.

  Since now efcap'd from what thou moft
    abhorr'ft——

LENA.

Efcap'd—Alas!——Has the poor hind e-
    fcap'd,
That flies, the barbed arrow in her heart?
Like her efcap'd, I feel like her the wound

Of certain death ; like her I only feek
Some quiet covert, there to die in peace !

ELFRIDA.

Let me through every defart go with thee,
And guard thee from this frenzy of defpair.

LENA.

Ah! find fome happier friend to fhare the blifs
Thy virtue merits.—Leave me and my forrows.

ELFRIDA.

Inhuman were the heart that thus could
leave thee !

LENA.

Sure thine is more than human! Generous
maid !
Has thy benevolence made thee forget .
What foes our fathers to each other were?

ELFRIDA.

But I fhall never be a foe to thee !

What

What though my father now leads on his
    bands
To affift Cadwallan!

LENA.

      Ha!—To affift that villain?
And cameft thou with that hoftile power?

ELFRIDA.

         A wifh
To fee this country, I fo much had heard of,
Brought me for once with armies to the field.
But fure fome power divine in fecret fped me
To refcue thee, while yet the tyrant flept.

LENA.

  O hadft thou come, when firft I call'd on
    heav'n
To fave me from difhonour, I had thought
    thee
One of its angels!——They, 'tis faid, have
    come,
In lovely forms like thine, to virtue's aid.—
But I'm unworthy of fuch care of heaven!

               ELFRIDA.

ELFRIDA.

Believe me, fent by heav'n to fave thee ftill!
My father will convey thee to thy Ofrick.

LENA.

Alas! who knows if yet my Ofrick lives!

ELFRIDA.

Have you not heard of him fince his defeat?

LENA.

My own afflictions followed that fo faft,
No time was giv'n me to enquire of him.
Bleeding at many wounds my father came!
Ere he could fpeak, this tyrant of the Britons,
Whofe love I had rejected, came enraged:
Ev'n in my arms he flew thee, O my father!
Prefent to me ftill feem thy dying pangs,
And thofe fad looks, which, after fpeech had
　　. fail'd,
Exprefs'd more ftrong than language could,
　　　thy fears,
Prophetic of my fate.

K　　　　　　　　SCENE

SCENE II.

Enter Hanna haſtily.

HANNA.

C ADWALLAN comes!

ELFRIDA.

Give me the cloaths.   But do not follow us,

LENA.

Protect me heavens!—Oh let ſome ravenous
    beaſt
Relieve me from this monſter more abhorr'd!

Exit with Elfrida.

HANNA *alone.*

I'll from a different quarter meet his ſight,
And by ſome falſe intelligence miſguide him.

Exit.

SCENE

SCENE III.

Enter Cadwallan and Brudus.

CADWALLAN.

Inform me, for you know, how she escap'd.

BRUDUS.

The Ladies of the Caftle, when they heard
Th' arrival of the daughter of your friend,
The King of Weffex, went and introduc'd her
In royal form. She ftaid not long within,
But walk'd forth to the garden with a train
Of many ladies. Among thofe we find
She had conceal'd the Princefs of Northum-
         bria.
They fled together by the lower gate
Into that wooded bank, that copfe, which winding
Along the river meets the foreft here.
They cannot yet be farther than——

CAD-

CADWALLAN.

You wiſh them——
Traitors! ye all conſpir'd againſt my peace!
And was it pity mov'd your ruffian hearts?
No! 'Twas ſedition!——Say, who murmur'd
  firſt?
But all ſhould ſuffer for the traiterous deed!

BRUDUS.

Let no ſuch thoughts diſturb your royal
  breaſt:
Your ſoldiers ſtill are faithful.

CADWALLAN.

Think'ſt thou ſo?
I'll ſearch however.——

BRUDUS.

Yonder! See my liege.

CADWALLAN.

Methought I ſaw a female form glide quick
Through yonder trees.——

      BRUDUS.

BRUDUS.

It was Elfrida's maid!

CADWALLAN.

Purfue you that way. I will guard this opening.

Exit Brudus.

I know not wherefore 'tis: But from this
  act,
By which I thought at once to gratify
My love and my revenge, my thoughts recoil,
In confcious ftarts; as from fome fhocking
  deed,
Some monftrous crime. When I expected
  blifs,
A fecret chilling horror through me ran,
Confounding every fenfe. Thou Judge fe-
  vere,
That hold'ft thy ftrict tribunal in our breafts!
'Twas thy juft fentence, which no wealth can
  bribe,
No power repel, no pleafure's opiate foothe.

SCENE

SCENE IV.

Enter Brudus with Hanna.

HANNA.

I KNOW not where they are.—I fought them
    here,
Becaufe I thought Elfrida, by this way,
Would lead th'unhappy Princefs to the place,
Where Kenwal is encampt.

CADWALLAN.

Is he fo near us?

HANNA.

We left him lately fcarce a mile from this.

CADWALLAN.

Have they not fled to him?

HANNA.

HANNA.

Alas! I know not.
But 'tis moſt probable.

CADWALLAN.

Then follow them.
Exit Hanna.

SCENE V.

CADWALLAN.

How am I chang'd!—Erewhile when I
was told,
That Kenwal came, my heart was wont to
leap,
Anticipating happineſs.——But now
I would avoid him.

BRUDUS.

Yet he brings thee aid!

CAD-

CADWALLAN, *walking aside.*

And why avoid him!—No. It is not fhame!
Is it remorfe?—For what?—I did no wrong!
Then what difturbs me?—Falfely we feek de-
    light
From pleafure's cup, when confcience taints
    the draught.

BRUDUS.

Why fhould you ftartle at a juft revenge?

CADWALLAN.

By heav'n, tis juft!——To be rejected,
    fcorn'd!
And for fo mean a rival; whofe bafe blood
No father owns.——'Twas difappointed love
Inflam'd to fury!—What is done, I did
In paffion. Cool reflection now condems it.
All will condemn it.—All my former friends
Will turn indignant from me.——Let them
    do fo!——
Think'ft thou that Kenwal will withhold his
    aid?

BRUDUS.

BRUDUS.

We need no aid of him to conquer Ofrick.

CADWALLAN.

I cannot, like a fuperftitious girl
To her confeffor, figh a piteous tale
Of human frailty, and implore forgivenefs.
Made of more ftubborn ftuff, my haughty
     heart,
That ill can bear ev'n friendfhip's kind re-
     buke,
Will fwell with ill-tim'd paffion, and convert
My friend into a foe.

BRUDUS.

     From that, I hope,
Your long-try'd friendfhip will fecure you
     both.

CADWALLAN.

Let us bring up our army ere we meet him.

L   BRUDUS.

BRUDUS.

'Twere beſt to meet him ſoon; ere ſlander's
    breath
Infect this action with a fouler ſtain.

Exeunt.

S C E N E VI.

Enter Lena and Elfrida, in mens cloaths.

ELFRIDA.

NOW they are gone. Come forward with
    aſſurance:
And ſince we have put on th' attire of men,
Let us endeavour to aſſume the looks
And fearleſs geſtures of the bolder ſex.

LENA.

Howe'er diſguis'd, my fears and ſorrows
    ſtill
Confeſs the female weakneſs of my heart!

HANNA.

HANNA *entering.*

Your father, Lady, and your brother come
This way on foot, advanc'd before their troops.
Exit.

ELFRIDA.

Then with them comes our safety.

LENA.

          Safety! Ha!
With whom? Alas! With Edwin's enemies!
And have they not combin'd with Ofrick's
     foes
For our deftruction? Where is then the hope,
The fole fad hope, that footh'd my mifery?
The hope of vengeance?

ELFRIDA.

         Know our fathers better!
Whilft emulous in the field, with ardour both
Aim'd, at their rivals, wounds, deftruction,
     death,

L 2   Reciprocal

Reciprocal efteem both bofoms warm'd;
And each had mourn'd his own compleat
    fuccefs.
'Tis true, Cadwallan is my father's friend,
And now expects th' affiftance of his force.
But when my father knows th' unworthy act
So late committed, he will change his pur-
    pofe.
Let us inform him of it.

LENA.

           Let me fly
From him, from all, to filence and defpair!
Shall I bow down before Cadwallan's friend?
And when I've, blufhing, told my fhameful
    tale,
Be fcorn'd, and fent, perhaps, a captive back!

ELFRIDA.

  So bafe an action never ftain'd his fame!
Diftrefs to Kenwal feldom fues in vain!
Remember we're difguifed! From Edwin
    fprung,
You fhall appear his fon. Without a blufh
              Relate

Relate to Kenwal no fictitious tale
Of Edwin's murder, and his daughter's
   wrongs.

LENA.

How can my fwelling heart and fault'ring
   tongue
Exprefs fuch wrongs! With more eafe thou
   may'ft tell it.
And if thy friendly bofom heave a figh,
Or eyes let fall a pitying tear for me,
'Twill give fuch graceful force to thy expref-
   fion,
As cannot fail to move a father's heart,
And turn it from a friend fo undeferving.

ELFRIDA.

Thou would'ft not then, it feems, remain
   unknown!

LENA.

Did that efcape me?——Known I muft not
   be!

ELFRIDA.

ELFRIDA.

My well-known voice would foon difcover
    us!
If you would be unknown, you muft attempt
To fpeak in this difguife like Edwin's fon.

LENA.

Muft I attempt it?

ELFRIDA.

                    Yes: If you would fave
Your hufband from deftruction, and yourfelf
From the detefted fate, which now you fly.

LENA.

For thofe great ends, wilt thou, my father's
    fpirit!
Who ftill perhaps behold'ft thy wretched
    daughter,
Forgive that daughter, when thou fec'ft her
    bow
To beg protection from thine enemy?

                              ELFRIDA.

ELFRIDA.

See they are here! Let us move towards
them.

SCENE VII.

To them enter Kenwal and Ofwald.

KENWAL.

Young warriors, ye appear as if ye had
Something of moment to inform us of.

LENA.

Great is the fame of Kenwal in the field;
But greater far compaſſion's nobleſt acts!
Diſtreſs, 'tis ſaid, ne'er pray'd to him in vain;
And oft his foes, when other hopes had fail'd,
Have found relief in his benevolence.
Confiding in that fame behold the fon
Of Edwin thy moſt hated enemy?

KENWAL.

KENWAL.

Thou Edwin's fon?——Rife, rife, and tell
    thy forrows
To me, who never did thy father hate.

LENA.

And if thou didft, 'tis time that hate fhould
    ceafe:
For Edwin now can injure thee no more!

KENWAL.

What mean thy words?—We heard of his
    defeat,
But not his death! In battle has he fall'n?

LENA.

They bore him from the battle to his for-
    trefs,
Wounded and feeble with the lofs of blood.
Cadwallan came, and in that very hall,
Where oft in feftive mirth they fat together,
He flew my father fainting in his wounds!

OSWALD.

OSWALD.

What? Faint with former wounds !——In
his own hall !
And when the rage of battle had fubfided ?

LENA.

Ev'n in his fhrieking daughter's arms he
flew him !

KENWAL.

Oh Edwin ! Edwin !——Whilft thou waft
in life,
I often wifh'd thee dead !——Witnefs thefe
tears,
It gives me now no joy !——Revenge, which
once
I thought a paffion worthy of the brave,
Seems now the bafeft vice of little minds !
What ! in his daughter's arms ! He ?——Cad-
wallan ?
Could he do this ?

M

LENA.

LENA.

Oh! had he done no worſe,
I never, never thus had ſued to thee!

KENWAL.

Wrong not my friend!—Though in reſentment fierce.
By honour's faireſt laws he ever liv'd;
And liv'd renown'd.   Worſe!—What could
he do worſe?

LENA.

One daughter Edwin had, by all eſteem'd
Of virtuous fame.——Forgive me—Oh! forgive me!

KENWAL.

He ſlew not her!

LENA.

Why, why, too rigid heav'n!
Was ſhe not doom'd to that far milder fate?
KENWAL.

KENWAL.

Command thy forrows till thy tale be told.

LENA.

Torn, while fhe clafp'd her murder'd fa-
ther's corfe,
And hither dragg'd by violence, fhe fuffer'd
The worft fhe could from cruelty and luft!

KENWAL.

How know you what the Princefs fuffer'd
there?

LENA.

A captive there, too well was I inform'd
Of her unhappy fate.

KENWAL.

Where is fhe now?

LENA.

Thy daughter, like an angel fent from
heav'n,

M 2

But

But ah! too late, to fave the innocent,
Came while Cadwallan flept.   Her generous
    heart
Was foften'd with th' account of Lena's
    wrongs:
She, with the ladies who had charge of her,
Led the unhappy Princefs to a garden,
Whence they together fled to come to you.

KENWAL.

To us they have not come.

LENA.

    Ha!——Have they not?
A confcious fhame perhaps keeps her con-
    ceal'd.

KENWAL.

You too were captives.—How did ye get
    free?

LENA.

We owe our fafety to your daughter too.

                 KENWAL.

KENWAL.

What? While Cadwallan flept?

LENA.

Yes! while he flept.

KENWAL.

Elfrida could not then folicit him :
And without his confent who durft releafe
    you?

LENA.

Thofe who had charge of us did venture it.

KENWAL.

'Twould be imprudent, youth, for us to
    give
An hafty credit to a tale like this,
Told by——no friend.

LENA.

Indeed I cannot boaft
Of being thy friend.—But in Elfrida's father

I

I thought to have found a generous mind like
    hers,
That would a little while protect a wretch,
Till Ofrick with his army came to fave me.

KENWAL.

Protection thou fhalt have: For though thy
    tale
Sounds fcarce like truth, I feel within my
    breaft
A tendernefs that wifhes to relieve thee.

LENA.

Our tale confirm'd will foon remove your
    doubts.

KENWAL *(to one of his officers.)*

Captain!—Conduct thefe Princes to our
    tent.
There let them be attended with refpect.
       [*Exeunt Lena and Elfrida attended.*

SCENE

S C E N E VIII.

KENWAL, OSWALD.

KENWAL.

I'LL not believe it. No! It muſt be falſe!

OSWALD.

Can you diſtruſt him? Surely from the
    heart
His ſorrow flow'd! With a more decent bluſh
Not Lena could relate her injuries.

KENWAL.

We know him not!——Be ſlow, my ſon,
    to truſt
The ſmootheſt tongue, when it reviles a
    friend:
Elſe you may curſe too late the fatal falſe-
    hood.

OSWALD.

OSWALD.

His years fpeak innocence; and in his
    looks
Appears the noble pride that fcorns deceit.

KENWAL.

Think you Cadwallan, like a prodigal,
Would, for a moment's pleafure, throw away
All the renown his life had treafur'd up?

OSWALD.

'Tis faid, that noble though he is, his paf-
    fions
Rule with no common force. He's forward,
    bold,
Impatient to poffefs what he defires;
Warm in his friendfhip, fierce in enmity,
And obftinately cruel in revenge.
When victory had put it in his pow'r
To gratify at once love and refentment;
What might he not?

KENWAL.

KENWAL.

I cannot think that he,
Mature in age, would by impetuous paſſion
Be hurried now to deeds of ignominy;
After his youth for almoſt half a life
Had been in ſolitude and ſorrow ſpent.

OSWALD.

Oft have I heard his ſufferings ſpoke of
thus,
As facts well-known: " How ſhort while af-
" ter marriage
" Had bleſt him with your faireſt ſiſter's
" charms,
" To ſhun the rage of ſtronger enemies,
" He was compell'd to plunge into the Severn,
" To ſwim aboard a veſſel, and in her
" Put off to ſea."—But why, or in what place,
He ſtaid ſo long, I ne'er diſtinctly heard.

KENWAL.

He reach'd the ſhip.——Deſerted of her
mariners

N   She

She in the eaftern gale and ebbing tide
Already ftretch'd her cable. That he fever'd.
Off flew the veffel.—Fierce the tempeft rofe,
And drove him helplefs o'er the fwelling bil-
     lows
Three days and ftormy nights. On the fourth
     morning
He faw the white waves wafh a rugged fhore,
At no great diftance. Right on that he fteer'd;
Dafh'd on the rocks; the planks afunder flew.
On one of thofe he floated to the fhore.
Climbing the rocks he found an ifle, where
     man
Had feldom trode. The cautious mariner
Avoids the dangerous coaft, where nature
     yields
Nought to allure his avarice. Yet there,
In want and folitude, he fofter'd life,
For fixteen tedious years.——Each morn he
     climb'd
The higheft land, and o'er the ocean look'd,
With wiftful gaze. At laft a bark appear'd,
Far in the Weft.—His eager fignal caught
The feaman's eye.—She boldly ftem'd the
     furge:

                       But

But bolder ftill, Cadwallan breafts the waves,
And gains her tow'ring fides.—Now fafe a-
  board,
The winds propitious waft the exile home
To Albion's land.——

OSWALD.

  But Emma was no more,
Ere he return'd?

KENWAL.

  You've often heard her fate.
His enemies, foon after his departure,
His caftle fir'd, and barb'roufly deftroyed
In it poor Emma, with her infant fon.——

OSWALD.

The light-arm'd bowmen, whom you fent
  before!

KENWAL.

Their fignals fpeak an enemy at hand!

      SCENE

SCENE IX.

(Enter an officer, with archers.)

OFFICER.

NOT diftant far, we through the trees de-
    fcry'd
An army well arrang'd. At firft we thought it
Cadwallan's hoft, and towards it advanc'd :
But, when within three arrow-flights, we
    knew
The bloody banners and the lengthen'd fpears
Of the Northumbrian front.

KENWAL.

      Call all to arms !
           [*Exeunt archers.*
In this oppreffive caufe I will not fight.

OSWALD.

What meafures will you then purfue ?
               KENWAL.

KENWAL.

                    I'll try
To mediate peace: Though fmall, I own, my
    hope
To reconcile fuch rivals, whofe fierce minds
Are fo incens'd by recent injuries.

OSWALD.

But, fince you hold the balance of their
    force,
Could you not make them finifh their difpute
By fingle combat?

KENWAL.

           Yes.—By that alone
It can be finifh'd.——One of them muft fall;
And by his death give life and peace to thou-
    fands.

              [*Alarm, and exeunt.*

END OF THE FIRST ACT.

                       ACT

A C T II.

SCENE I. A WOOD.

(Enter Osrick and Anfrid, with soldiers bring-
ing in two of the Britons prisoners.)

ANFRID.

WERE ye sent hither to explore our force?

FIRST PRISONER.

We were commanded in this wood to
    search
For the Northumbrian Princess, who this
    morning
Made her escape.

OSRICK.

My Princess!—She escap'd

SECOND

SECOND PRISONER.

Yes.—The Northumbrian Princeſs.

OSRICK.

In·this wood?

SECOND PRISONER.

We ſaw them to this foreſt aim their courſe.

OSRICK.

Saw *them*?—By whom is ſhe accompany'd?

FIRT PRISONER.

Elfrida, daughter of the King of Weſſex,
Came while Cadwallan ſlept, and ſtole her off.

OSRICK.

The daughter of the King of Weſſex ſav'd
her?

FIRST PRISONER.

Yes: And 'tis thought that in her father's
camp
They both are ſafe.

OSRICK.

OSRICK.

Great Governor of all!
Accept my thanks!—Protect my wife, and bless
This generous daughter of mine enemy!

ANFRID.

A trumpet sounds!

OSRICK.

Remove the prisoners.
They are led out.
See what this means.

AN OFFICER *(entering.)*

One from the King of Wessex;
Who in his right hand waves the branch of
peace,
And in his left a spear.

OSRICK.

Let him come forward.
He by his signals comes to offer peace
Upon

Upon conditions.   Well, I fear, he knows
To make advantage of this incident!
My Queen his captive! What can be too much
For Lena's ransom?

SCENE II.

(Enter Ofwald with attendants.)

OSWALD.

To Northumbria's Prince
The King of Weffex wifhes health and peace.

OSRICK.

From the Weft-Saxon King we look'd for
        war;
'Though more we wifh for peace—on equal
        terms.

OSWALD.

This Kenwal bids me tell thee.   He fore-
        fees

O   The

The certain issue of these hostile broils,
In wide-spread ruin: He laments its cause:
He sees with pain the sons of this fair isle
Waste in domestic wars their common force;
Which, if united, might have rais'd their
     country
To be the dread and envy of the world.

OSRICK.

I never with the Briton can unite.

OSWALD.

So Kenwal fears: For not unknown to him
Is the fell rancour that inflames you both.
But since, says he, the wrong is personal,
Since each avows his purpose in this war
To be the death and ruin of his foe;
Involve not guiltless thousands in the ven-
     geance;
But let the rival Kings themselves atchieve
This bloody purpose with their single swords.

OSRICK.

Our single swords!—Oh 'tis my keenest wish!

Let

Let Kenwal bring Cadwallan to my fword,
I afk no more. Then one or both fhall fall!
And all in Albion may like brothers join
To ftrike a terror in the nations round.

OSWALD.

In yonder wood, between your hoft and
    ours,
There is a deep recefs.—It has been nam'd
The trav'ller's couch; (for nature feems t'have
    deck'd
And fown its clofe green turf with fweeteft
    flow'rs,
For the relief of weary travellers.)
There, at the foot of a tall fpreading oak,
Which near its middle fingly fhades the
    ftream,
You'll find the King of Weffex. He entreats
That you without delay will meet him there,
To ratify the articles of combat.

OSRICK.

I go with fpeed.

OSWALD.

Take but along with you
Some chosen friends and guards,—I am his
    son;
And am commanded with your troops to stay
Till your return, an hostage for your safety.

OSRICK.

Son of a gallant father! I embrace thee
With true affection.——Anfrid, let the Prince
Be entertain'd with the distinction due
To his high rank, and with thy best regard.
Yes, noble youth, all gratitude is due
To him whose sister sav'd my hapless queen.

OSWALD.

Had they, as we expected, reach'd our
    camp,
It now had been my fortune to restore
Thy Princess to her Lord.

OSRICK.

Not reach'd your camp?
                            OSWALD.

Not when I left it.——

Ha!—Where are they then?

We thought t' have found them under your
   protection.

They are together still!—But how?—Per-
   haps,
Again his captives!——Or through devious
   wilds,
Mistaking us for enemies, they fly,
Ready to drop fatigu'd, or faint with fear,
At ev'ry waving bush or rustling leaf.
Send out strong parties. Leave no grove un-
   search'd
Till ye have found your Queen—How did
   you hear
Of their escape?

OSWALD.

'Twas from the son of Edwin:
For he too had escap'd captivity,
And to my father came with confidence.

OSRICK.

The son of Edwin?——Edwin left no son!

OSWALD.

He left no son?——What! Could so young
     a boy
Be an impostor? Thy suspicion guess'd
Aright, my father! Age is ever cautious.

OSRICK.

Edwin had but one son; the gallant Os-
     frid:
Him, brave beyond the promise of his
     years,
I saw in battle fall by mortal wounds.

OSWALD.

OSWALD.

The boy then play'd it well. He told a
tale
That mov'd us much. I'm pleas'd to find it
falfe.

OSRICK.

What tale told he?

OSWALD.

'Twould lofe your time to hear it.

OSRICK.

True! an impoftor's tale deferves no credit.

OSWALD. *(to fome of his attendants.)*

Conduct brave Ofrick to the trav'ller's
couch.

[*Exeunt feverally.*

SCENE

SCENE III.

THE TRAVELLER's COUCH.

CADWALLAN, KENWAL, AND ATTENDANTS.

KENWAL.

Yes——As your friends regret your mur-
    der'd fame,
Your enemies fhall, with exulting joy,
Receive and fpread this tale of your difho-
    nour.

CADWALLAN.

Who taxes me with deeds difhonourable?
Am I grown weak with age? Whoe'er before
Affail'd my honour, to his forrow felt,
My arm had pow'r that honour to defend.

KENWAL.

Can fear of greatnefs, power, or valour fi-
    lence

                 The

The voice of Rumour? Like the wind, it fwells
From the low whifper to the breeze; like
    wind,
It flies abroad; and, like the tempeft, beats
With greateft fury on the higheft tow'r.
But firm on virtue's bafe the good man ftands
Unmov'd, and fmiles at all its idle rage.
So once Cadwallan ftood!

CADWALLAN.

        And fo fhall ftand!
And ftill with force fhall hurl fuch tempefts
    back
Againft the flanderous mouths that utter
    them.
But wherefore am I blam'd?——Was I not
    injur'd?
Injur'd, how much!—And yet not half re-
    veng'd.

KENWAL.

Revenge let Ofrick feek.——He fuffer'd
    moft.

CADWALLAN.

Doft thou too favour him? Ev'n thou,
    my friend?
That fordid beggar's fpurious progeny,
Whofe unknown parents caft him out to
    ftarve,
Is ftill preferr'd to me, whofe fathers reign'd
In Albion, ere fhe was by Saxons plunder'd.

KENWAL.

Unknown although we grant this youth's
    defcent,
Report, in fpite of vulgar prejudice,
Allows him all the virtues of the mind,
That beft adorn a throne; proclaims him fuch
As greateft Princes wifh their fons to be.

CADWALLAN.

And fuch you wifh your friend.

KENWAL.

        'Tis true, I own,
I'd count his friendfhip of no common price.

CAD-

CADWALLAN.

Again I'm left for him!——Go to your
    friend!
Your honourable friend,—from nothing
    fprung!
'Tis war when next we meet.

[Going.

KENWAL.

Stay, madman, ftay.

CADWALLAN.

Provoke my wrath no farther!—For I
    would not
Cancel at once the bonds of antient amity.

SCENE

SCENE IV.

*(Enter Lena and Elfrida in their mens habits,
and stand aside among the officers attending.)*

KENWAL.

HEAR how I purpose to befriend thee.——

CADWALLAN.

No.——

An honeſt foe profeſt I do not hate,
Ev'n while I ſtrive to ward his angry blows.
But when I find a ſmooth, a ſmiling traitor,
Who under friendſhip's fair attire would hide
The dagger of his ſecret enmity,
To give a villain's ſtab; I hate him, ſcorn
    him;
As I do Kenwal now.

KENWAL.

       'Twas oft thy curſe,
          When

When fome imagin'd infult gall'd thy pride,
To treat thy beft of friends with fcorn and
    hate.

LENA *(afide.)*

Ye Pow'rs of Difcord! blow your poifon-
    ing blafts!

CADWALLAN.

No friend of mine can be the friend of Of-
    rick.

KENWAL.

Were he thy friend, that fhould perfuade
    that Prince
To fet the iffue of this threat'ning war
Upon his fingle fword to thine?

CADWALLAN.

           My friend!
By all my hopes of conqueft and revenge,
He, who did this, were as a god to me!

KENWAL.

KENWAL.

This Kenwal, whom you scorn and hate,
  has done.

LENA *(aside.)*

If e'er almighty Pow'r has interpos'd
In human actions——Have I found it so?

CADWALLAN *(aside.)*

I've been too hot! And yet my stubborn
  pride
Will not permit me to acknowledge it.

KENWAL.

Do you decline the combat?

CADWALLAN.

      Can'st thou think so?——
Could'st thou not for a moment bear my
  weaknefs?

KENWAL.

I've borne it long.

CADWALLAN.

Have we not long been friends?

KENWAL.

Let us be ſo for ever.

SCENE. V.

(*Enter Oſrick and attendants.*)

ONE OF THE ATTENDANTS.

NOrthumbria's Prince!

LENA (*aſide to Elfrida.*)

Support me, my Elfrida!

KENWAL.

Prince of Northumbria, we give thee welcome!

OSRICK.

OSRICK.

I come, O King! obedient to the meſſage
You ſent me by your ſon.——The Briton
    here!
Such enemies ſhould never meet, but thus!
           [*Drawing his ſword.*

CADWALLAN, (*drawing likewiſe.*)

And ſo I meet thee!

KENWAL.

Hold! I charge you both.

CADWALLAN.

Ha! wherefore hold?

KENWAL.

He who advances renders me his foe.

CADWALLAN.

Wherefore this ſtop? Did you not tell me
    now,

                    That

That th' iſſue of this threat'ning war was ſet
Upon our ſingle ſwords?

KENWAL.

So 'tis reſolv'd.

OSRICK.

And why not now; while my reſentment
    burns
To ſtrike this murderer?

CADWALLAN.

I ſcorn to anſwer thee.
Ev'n that were too much honour for a ſlave,
Of parentage unknown.

KENWAL.

Sheathe both your ſwords;
And let reſentment pauſe, till ye have heard
The reaſons which have made me wiſh to ſee
This war decided by a ſingle combat.

OSRICK, *(ſheathing his ſword.)*
You are obey'd.

Q.

CAD.

CADWALLAN, (*doing the fame.*)

Now let us hear thofe reafons.

KENWAL.

You fee our ifland in itfelf is bleft
With every requifite to man's content.
Did nature's God from ev'ry other land
Thus fever it by wide tempeftuous feas,
And gird it with its rocky walls t' inclofe
Barbarians, who fhould prey on one another?
Were ftrength and valour giv'n us to defeat
The great Creator's bleffings?—Surely not!—
Oft have I heard, or thought I heard, the
    Genius
Of Albion thus admonifhing her fons:
" Your feas and rocks, while your undaunted
    " hearts
" Join in your country's caufe, ye Britons,
    " fhall
" Defend you from th'affaults of foreign foes.
" But fhould diffention raife th' unnatural
    " rage
" Of mutual flaughter in your valiant breafts,
              " They

" They but drive back the weak on fure de-
　　" ftruction.

" Hence learn to live in concord, and improve

" The arts of peace.　Here, as in one great
　　" houfe,

" You live, like children of one family:

" So you, like brothers, fhould join all your
　　" ftrength

" To guard your common goods from out-
　　" ward force,

" Or check the progrefs of domeftic rapine.

CADWALLAN.

Had th' antient fons of Britain fo united,
No tyrant Saxon e'er had fill'd her throne.

KENWAL.

We fee their errors, but avoid them not!
Ev'n now, we know the envious nations
　　round us,
Watching th' event of thefe imprudent wars,
Rejoice to fee our folly fight their battles,
And long to feize their felf-defeated prey.
Princes of Albion! in that common name

Be

Be every national diftinction loft!
Scorning all lefs ambition, let us ftrive,
Beft to defend, embellifh, and exalt
Our common country. 'Twas this patriot
      wifh
Which prompted that decifion, I have nam'd,
Of thofe fell contefts, elfe to be bequeath'd,
From fire to fon, till univerfal wafte
Depopulate fair Albion's fertile vales.
This to prevent, let all your chiefs agree,
That howfoe'er this combat terminate,
They fhall immediately difband their troops,
And live in peace hereafter.

CADWALLAN.

Be it fo!

OSRICK.

. Then call our captains——They will now
    confent.

KENWAL.

Proclaim't to either hoft!——All muft con-
    fent:

                        All

All be fpectators of th' important combat;
That no contention afterwards may rife
From falfe report.—Go bring your marfhall'd
 bands
Into the open field without their arms.
There front to front oppos'd, as if prepar'd
For battle, let them ftand three bow-fhot dif-
 tant.
Mine arm'd, in two divifions will I place
On either flank; and, in the midft, the chiefs
Of all our hofts fhall form a fpacious ring.
There, Princes, you on equal terms fhall fight
To mortal iffue!——May the God of battles
Direct that dread event to Britain's weal!

CADWALLAN.

Come, let us inftantly prepare for it!
     [Exit with his train.

SCENE

SCENE VI.

KENWAL, OSRICK, LENA, ÈLFRIDA, ETC.

KENWAL.

'TIS ſtrange Cadwallan neither knew his
    captive,
Nor Oſrick Edwin's ſon!

OSRICK.

        Ha! where is he?
Who dar'd aſſume that ſacred name?

KENWAL.

        This youth,

OSRICK.

Too young impoſtor! Edwin left no ſon!
His only ſon before his father fell!

KENWAL.

KENWAL.

I did fufpect him.   Now I find him falfe,
O could I likewife find the ftory falfe
He told of Lena!

OSRICK.

How?—What ftory? Ha!——
Was it not him who told of her efcape?
What told he more?—What has fhe fuffer'd?
    fpeak!
Why doft thou tremble? Wherefore turn from
    me?——
Oh Kenwal! tell me all: I am prepar'd
To hear the worft. Speak out and end my
    mifery.

KENWAL.

Can I repeat, or you believe the words
Of one convicted of fuch grofs impofture?

OSRICK.

So! 'tis, it feems, too dreadful for my hear-
    ing!
                    Speak,

Speak, gentle youth! I have forgiv'n thy
    fraud;
Thy harmlefs fraud: I fwear I will not hurt
    thee.
Tell, tell me all! It cannot how exceed
The apprehenfion of a fond, fond hufband!
What doft thou know of Lena?

LENA *(fainting.)*

Oh! too much!

ELFRIDA.

Help, help me to fupport my fainting
    friend!

KENWAL.

What fcene have thefe impoftors now to
    play?

OSRICK.

Sure no impofture could affect me fo!

ELFRIDA,

ELFRIDA (*difcovering herfelf.*)

There's no impofture!——Edwin was her father!
And Kenwal mine!

KENWAL.

Elfrida!

OSRICK.

O my Lena!
She ftirs not! breathes not!—Art thou gone for ever?

KENWAL.

Let us retire. The anguifh of this fcene
Bears not a ftranger's prefence.

[*Exit with his attendants.*

R   SCENE

SCENE VII.

OSRICK, LENA, ELFRIDA.

OSRICK, *(holding her.)*

SHE breathes! She lives!

LENA, *(recovering.)*

Begone, vile murderer!
Hence, murderer of the beſt of fathers!

OSRICK.

Why doſt thou talk ſo wildly?——'Tis thy
Oſrick.

LENA.

My Oſrick! Yes, 'tis he.——Where have
I been?

OSRICK.

I tremble ſtill! We thought thee gone forever!

LENA.

LENA.

Why, why did I revive?

OSRICK.

T' adorn the world,
And blefs the fondeft hufband.——

LENA.

Oh, no more!
With me you never can be happy more!

OSRICK.

What means my love? Speak, fpeak, my
Lena! tell me!——
Let me no more be torn with dire furmifes!

LENA.

Fly me! O heav'ns! unworthy now thy
fight!
Fly me polluted!——

OSRICK.

Ha! Polluted!—How?

R 2

LENA.

By force!——The villain!——

OSRICK.

No! impoſſible!
Cadwallan!—Monſter! Were it as thou ſay'ſt,
Hell has no puniſhment for ſuch a fiend!

LENA.

Oh me! too true.——My tongue denies to
ſpeak it.

OSRICK.

Then ſince thy lightning ſpar'd the monſter's head,
Hear me, juſt heav'n! while Oſrick has a
thought,
That thought muſt be of Lena and revenge!

LENA.

My wiſhes all, like thine are for revenge!
But—in my fancy lately there aroſe
A terror, which confounds me!

OSRICK.

OSRICK.

Speak it out.

LENA.

Then think not harfhly of a woman's fears.
We've heard, that the defcendants of the
    wicked
Are often punifh'd for their parents crimes!
You know not yet ('tis hence my terrors rife)
The blood which gave you birth.   What if
    you find it
Ally'd to him?

OSRICK.

There is no caufe to think fo?

LENA.

Perhaps there is not.——But while both
    ftood here,
Burning with rage, and threatning fell re-
    venge;
I thought I faw that likenefs in your looks
Which marks the kindred features.

OSRICK.

OSRICK.

Let not this
Imaginary phantom aggravate
Your real forrows! Groundlefs 'tis and vain!

LENA.

Vain as it is, it will not from my mind!
Threat echo'd threat, and frown refembled
  frown,
As juftly as the image in the pool
Reflects the paffing cloud that fhadows it.

OSRICK.

But though I were ally'd to him, could that
Reftrain refentment, or avert my rage?
No!—Though one mother at one ominous
  hour
Had to the world produc'd us, Lena's wrongs
Would juftify the moft compleat revenge.

LENA.

Had you been brothers! Heav'ns! how
  that alarms me!
         OSRICK.

OSRICK.

Since reafon's earlieft dawn my ftrongeft
    wifh
Has been to know my parents!—Hear, great
    Pow'r!
Whofe awful vengeance trembling mortals
    fear!
Hear, and record in folemn form this vow!
" To all intelligence of my defcent,
" Left that fhould crofs my purpofe, I'll be
    " deaf,
" Till in his hated blood I glut revenge.
" This if I fail in, write my perjur'd name
" In the curft roll of black Perdition's fons.

LENA.

May'ft thou return with glorious vic-
    tory!
O may the gods preferve that precious life,
For a long train of blifsful years to come,
For happinefs which I muft never tafte!

OSRICK.

What does my Lena mean? Unkind! Thou
 know'ft
Without thee I have neither joy nor hope.

LENA.

Henceforth no joy no hope remains for
 me!
Oh could I find in fome far-diftant wild,
Amidft the favage rocks, fome difmal cave,
So deeply funk that yet no daring mortal
Has ever founded its tremendous gloom,
Defperate, I'd plunge into its fartheft horrors;
And then implore its rugged jaws to clofe,
To hide forever an ill-fated wretch,
The tale of fools, the fcorn of fhamelefs
  dames,
A torment to herfelf and all who love her!

ELFRIDA, (coming forward.)

Divert her, Ofrick, from this fatal purpofe.

          OSRICK.

OSRICK.

What dreadful refolution lurks within
My Lena's breaft?

LENA.

Shall Lena live in fhame?

OSRICK.

Would you deprive me of the only hope
That could fupport me in the hour of danger!
For what is vengeance, victory, or fame,
When there's no Lena to partake the joy?

LENA.

Could'ft thou behold the anguifh of my
    foul,
Ev'n thou, in pity, wouldft prefent a dagger;
And bid me purchafe reft!

OSRICK.

Moft fhocking thought!

S   Heav'ns!

Heav'ns !——Ev'ry word you utter in this
    ftrain,
Sharp as a dagger, wounds me to the heart!
Yet I for thee could fuffer worfe than death!

LENA.

And worfe than death for thee I'll ftrive to
    fuffer.
A life of fhame is worfe, far worfe than
    death.

OSRICK.

Ah! if thou lov'ft me, give me caufe to hope,
That, when I have reveng'd our injuries,
Time may efface remembrance, and reftore
My Lena's peace, and with it all my blifs.

LENA.

Hope all my refolution can perform.

OSRICK.

Heav'n ftrengthen that, and we again are
    bleft.——

                            Thou

Thou fair, thou kind deliverer of my Queen!
Be ſtill her guardian angel.—Leave her not
While ſhe is anxious for this great event.

ELFRIDA.

Yes, truſt her to my care.—If friendſhip's
    pow'r,
If ſympathy can ſoothe her troubled mind,
What claim can equal Lena's on Elfrida?

OSRICK.

Moſt generous Princeſs! May the God of
    juſtice
Reward thy virtue with the bliſs it merits!
See, Anfrid brings a party to conduct
Us to our camp.　Let us advance to meet
    him.

             [*Exeunt.*

END OF THE SECOND ACT.

　　　　　　　ACT

ACT III.

SCENE I.

A Cave in a Rock.

Enter Ofrick and Anfrid.

OSRICK.

HAVE I been here before ?——I dream not
   now !——
Amazing prodigy !—Evil or good
Uncommon it portends !

ANFRID.

   What ftrikes thee fo ?

OSRICK.

I ne'er was here before, and yet this place,
         Thofe

Thofe rocks, thofe trees, that cave appear as
    things
With which my mind has been familiar
    long:
For oft have I beheld them in my dreams,
Diftinct as now I fee them.

ANFRID.

                     Can it be?
Then, fure, thy mind look'd forward to this
    combat,
Which, whether profperous or not, becomes
The moft important action of thy life.

OSRICK.

Dreams us'd not to affect me.—But this
    cave
Brings to my memory a fcene whofe hor-
    rors
Made deep impreffion. 'Twas one folemn
    night;
(One of thofe nights, in which 'tis thought
    the faints
Defcend with heav'n's behefts to pious men;)
                        That

When I, with more than common warmth,
    had pray'd,
That God would fend my foul fome inward
    light,
About the blood from which my being came:
In fuch a cave as this, beneath fuch clifts,
And fhaded by fuch boughs, methought I
    found
A venerable man.   Him foon I knew
To be the father I had often fought.
I ran t' embrace him with a fon's affection:
He feem'd to dafh againft me, like a wave:
From which, methought, a black, foul river ran:
Down this foul current feem'd to float the
    fhades
Of drown'd, or drowning wretches: Among
    thefe,
I faw my Lena ftruggling ftill for life.
I ftrove to refcue her.—I funk myfelf.
Then horror wak'd me.

ANFRID, *(going towards the cave.)*

        We will fee this cave!
Does any living thing inhabit here!

                SCENE

SCENE II.

DRUID, *(from the cave entering.)*

TH' indulgent Gods preferve me ftill in
life.

ANFRID.

Had the heav'n-created father of mankind
Surviv'd till now, he could not have look'd
older !

OSRICK.

Art thou a creature of this earth? Or fent
From heav'n to Ofrick?

DRUID.

And art thou Prince Ofrick?
Th' adopted Son of the Northumbrian King?

OSRICK.

I am that Ofrick: Now Northumbria's
King !

DRUID.

DRUID.

And has my aged fight remain'd to fee thee
Reftor'd, in manhood, to that princely rank.
From which, an infant, thou waft forc'd a-
  way?

OSRICK.

For heav'n's fake, what art thou that
  know'ft fo much?

DRUID.

A creature of this earth; fo worn with
  years,
That to exprefs my nature would require
A name lefs dignify'd than that of man.

OSRICK.

What waft thou in thy youth?

DRUID.

     I was a Druid:
And ftill, adhering to my native faith,

I

I worſhip and adore one God of all,
By the ſame rites our firſt forefathers us'd.

ANFRID.

I thought that ſect had long ſince died
away.

DRUID.

My youth beheld its antient prieſts expire,
The young embrace the faſhionable zeal
Of Chriſtians.   Conſtant to my ſacred vows;
For many years I, almoſt ſingly, ſtood
Againſt the progreſs of that novel faith.
Finding my ſtruggles vain, myſelf forſaken,
And forc'd th' unequal conflict to decline,
I hither from the ſcoffing world retir'd.
Full fourſcore winters, in this lonely dwell-
ing,
Have I, with fruitleſs ſorrow, mourn'd the
change.

OSRICK.

And has the God, whom thou doſt ſerve,
reveal'd

T   To

To thee alone the fecret of my birth?
How could'ft thou elfe, me, or my fortunes
   know?

DRUID.

Twice ten times has that oak renew'd his
   fhade,
Since thy fair mother with her infant fon,
Thyfelf, came hither.—" Wretched babe,"
   fhe cry'd,
" I have preferv'd thee from their cruel
   " fwords,
" From flames, at midnight rais'd for horrid
   " ends."——

OSRICK.

No more!—I'll hear no more.—My ears
   are fhut!
I find thou know'ft the ftory of my birth.—
Seal yet awhile thy lips, thou holy man,
To that myfterious fecret.——I have fworn
This day to reft in ignorance.—This day
Fills up the crifis of my fate.—I'll hear
At my return whate'er thou haft to tell.

                              [*Exeunt.*
                              SCENE

SCENE III.

DRUID, (*alone.*)

Never was day of forrows ufher'd in
With more ill-boding prodigies. When firft
I view'd the dawning of the morn, it
    feem'd
A vault of variegated flame, and caft
O'er hills and woods a difmal bloody hue:
While, like a ftream of gore, burft from the
    rocks,
Appear'd yon rapid rill, which down their
    cliffs,
Now white as fnow, comes rufhing to the
    valley.
This oak, long reverenc'd by holy Druids,
Without a breeze through all its branches
    fhook,
The huge trunk trembled;—and its yet young
    leaves
Fell faft, as in the firft froft's nipping blafts.

Before

Before my cave a fox had feiz'd a fawn:
Th' impatient mother ran to its relief;
Her erring aim flew him fhe meant to fave;
And foon herfelf became th' affailant's prey!
So the miftaken mother of this Prince,
Where fhe defign'd his fafety, brought his
    ruin.

SCENE IV.

Enter Cadwallan and Ofwald.

OSWALD.

HA! who is yonder venerable man?

CADWALLAN.

An antient Druid, laft of all his race;
Himfelf the fole furviving monument
Of that extinguifh'd faith.—Twice has he told
The natural age of man; yet found his mind,
And vigorous yet his frame: Such the re-
    ward

Of

Of virtuous temperance, of a life fo pure,
As had done honour to the beft religion.

DRUID.

Health, honour, power, content, and peace
of mind,
Blefs long the days and nights of Britain's
King !

CADWALLAN.

Thanks, reverend Druid.——What haft
thou with me ?

DRUID.

Let not, my Liege, an unjuft prejudice
Againft the faith of Druids, fhut thine ear
To the found counfel of far-fighted age.

CADWALLAN.

Whate'er thy counfel, thou mayft freely
fpeak.

DRUID.

Then do not fight.——Defeat or victory
Alike

Alike are fatal. Thence deftruction comes
To thee or thine.

CADWALLAN.

What demon told thee this?

DRUID.

No demon, Sir,—no fupernatural pow'r!
I fpeak from certain knowledge of the paft.

CADWALLAN.

Whate'er thy knowledge be, I heed it not.
For now to end this war, I go to meet
My hated rival in a fingle combat.

DRUID.

O Britain's King, for whofe profperity
I lift thefe aged hands in earneft prayer,
With each day's rifing and declining light!
Shun, I befeech thee, fhun this dreadful
  combat.

CADWALLAN.

Think not t' enfnare me, Druid, by fuch arts
          As

As crafty priefts of falfe religions ufe
T' intimidate the fuperftitious mind :
For I regard no prophecies, no dreams,
No fecrets told by vifionary faints.

DRUID.

Avoid this combat.——But enquire no
    more.

CADWALLAN.

Firft you muft tell me why I fhould avoid
    it.

DRUID.

That I have fworn that I would never tell.

CADWALLAN.

What!—Sworn!—To whom? Some dif-
    contented flave,
Who has confpir'd againft my life or pow'r?
Doft thou refufe t' obey the King's com-
    mands,
And fear'ft thou not the torture?

                    DRUID.

DRUID.

Torture!—No!
Have you not known me yet?——Then know
    me now!
In life's gay fpring, when at the touch of joy
The ready-kindling fpirits quickly flafh
In fweeteft raptures through the glowing
    nerves,
Difdaining pleafures, wealth, and proffer'd
    pow'r,
Rather than violate my vows, I chofe
This life of poverty, and man's contempt.
Were not thefe worfe to bear than death or
    torture?
Now age, the winter of man's life, has frozen
Each channel of delight in thefe cold limbs.
I've fcarce a wifh for life;—for death no ter-
    ror.

CADWALLAN.

Thou ever waft efteem'd a wond'rous man,
Whom human hopes or fears affected little.
But death and torture make the boldeft fhake.
                  And

And thofe canft thou, fo worn with age defpife ?

DRUID.

Some fools, whofe fpirits with their limbs
decay,
Grow fonder ftill of life, as that grows worth-
lefs.
But think not I am fuch.——No, no, my
King !
Now life to me is like a tedious tale
Oft heard before : I long for its conclufion.
Serene in torture, I fhould fmile to think—
" Now I fhake off this load of wretchednefs !
" Now, now, I haften to applauding gods !

CADWALLAN.

Already thou feem'ft more than man ! Divine
Thou groweft as thy mortal parts decay !
And doft thou, like a God, fee things before
Their forms are vifible to human fight ?

DRUID.

This I can fee: That if thou fight with Ofrick,

U   Fatal

Fatal that fight will prove!

CADWALLAN.

To me, or mine?
Such were thy former words.

DRUID.

And prefent thoughts,

CADWALLAN.

Whom call'ft thou mine?—For children
now nor wife,
Nor parent, brother, kindred have I none.

DRUID.

Thou hadft a wife and fon.

CADWALLAN.

Alas! I had!——
But have no more!—You knew their dreadful fate!

OSWALD.

OSWALD.

I've heard that they were in their caſtle
    burnt,
While thou, far diſtant on a deſart iſland,
With many hardſhips ſtruggled all alone.

CADWALLAN.

Yes.——In my abſence I did ſuffer much:
But more,—much more, when I arriv'd at
    home.

OSWALD.

And thoſe more bitter, as you hop'd for
    joy.

CADWALLAN.

With what glad raptures did I hail the
    light
Of that long-wiſh'd-for morning, which diſ-
    play'd
The diſtant veſſel's ſail;—when from the
    waves

          The

The mariners receiv'd me!——Profperous
     gales
Soon brought me joyful to my native ftream.
'Twas midnight when I came afhore. Elate
With ev'ry tender hope of wife and fon,
I painted to myfelf their fweet diftrefs
In the firft tranfports of unhop'd-for joy!
But, oh!—how different was the fcene I
     found!

OSWALD.

Ah!—Had you never heard of their dif-
    aftre?

CADWALLAN.

Not, till I faw it in my caftle's ruin.——
I went to the next cottage. There a ftrippling
Scoff'd at my raggednefs. But round my
     neck,
His well-known mafter's neck, the father
     flew.——
Enquiring of my Emma, I was told,
She and her fon, when now his thoughtlefs
     fmiles

                          Had

Had juft begun to foothe her widowed forrow,
Perifh'd (oh horror!) in devouring fire!

DRUID.

Perhaps they dy'd not there.

CADWALLAN.

                    They dy'd not there!
Why then, they ftill may live!

DRUID.

                    Enquire no more.————
For yet I dare not fpeak.   Defer this combat,
Till twice the fun fhall warm the weftern
            waves;
And————thou may'ft hear————

CADWALLAN.

          Of Emma fhall I hear?

DRUID.

Defer the combat,—and thou may'ft— be
    happy.

CADWALLAN.

Defer the combat!——Ha!—To hear of
 Emma!
For that vain hope, vain though I think it be,
What would I not ?——I'd beg my life of Of-
 rick!
I'd give that flave my kingdom!——I would
 fly
From the lov'd buftle of th' embattled field,
And let report arraign me for a coward!

 [*Exit with Ofwald.*

SCENE V.

DRUID, (*alone.*)

WERE it not better yet to follow him,
And tell him all? To this humanity
Inclines: But from that facred oak a voice
Of more than human found, methinks, ex-
 claims:
" Poor fon of earth! think not t' elude thy God!
 " That

" That God, who hates the perjur'd, fees thee
    " now !
" What thou haft promis'd in his fight, per-
    " form ;
" Though there deftruction feem to gape for
    " thee!
" What God refolves can he not bring about,
" Without thy feeble aid !"——Almighty
    Pow'r!
Thy will be done ! But O enlight my foul
By fome fure impulfe : Such as oft I've felt
When thus diftracted with important doubts.
Upon my couch I'll wait thy vifitation.

    [Goes into his cave.

S C E N E VI.

Enter Emma and Etha.

EMMA.

THAT cave of devils !—Has it yet efcap'd
Th' avenging bolt ?

    ETHA.

ETHA.

Alas! you make me fear
Your brain's diforder'd !—Could this cave offend you ?

EMMA.

There was my fatal refolution form'd !
My vow imprudent!——If you knew the
caufe,
You'd wonder at my patience.

ETHA.

What it was
That made you to the world prefer the con-
vent,
I never yet could learn.——When firft you
came,
You chofe me for your friend; and oft though I
Surprifing you in tears, enquir'd the caufe;
You only anfwer'd me with filent groans.
Your grief was recent then; and yet you
feem'd
Refign'd with patience to the will of heav'n.

Amaz'd

Amaz'd I now fee your affliction's wounds,
After they feem'd by twenty fummers heal'd,
Burft out at once without apparent caufe!
Frantic and wild, you fudden call on me,
By all our friendfhip, at the midnight hour,
To follow thee.——I know not why or whi-
    ther!

EMMA.

Thy love, indeed, deferv'd more confi-
    dence.
Forgive me; for I thought my reafons good,
I find I was deceiv'd.

ETHA.

Deceiv'd?—By whom?

EMMA.

Hell's minifters, by true religion driven
From holy fanes, fled with their Druids hither,
And round this curfed cave they hover'd long,
To ruin wretches who confided in them.
Deceiv'd by them, I never told my ftory.

X

Scarce

Scarce dare I yet difclofe it; though I find
That to obey thofe demons is perdition.

ETHA.

You make me more impatient ftill to hear
Your ftory told.

EMMA.

Oh!—Had I told it fooner,
I had not been thus wretched!

ETHA.

Tell it now.

EMMA.

Here dwelt a Druid.   Wifdom ftamp'd
            with age,
And firm integrity, made him rever'd.
But fome infernal demon 'twas, that there
He for a god ador'd!—For, fure, from hell,
Malicious hell, arofe that dream, which
            caus'd
The miferies of Emma?——By that name
                                Well

Well was the Queen of brave Cadwallan
 known.——

ETHA.

Thou Emma!—Heav'ns!—The great Cadwallan's Queen?

EMMA.

That wretch (too fure!) am I.

ETHA.

     Then by what chance
Didft thou efcape the flames?—For fhe, 'twas
 faid,
Was with her infant fon burnt in their caftle.

EMMA.

So 'twas believ'd; nor could my friends
 conceive,
From any circumftance, the fmalleft hope.
At midnight blaz'd the caftle all around us;
And cruel murd'rers watch'd at ev'ry gate.
Death feem'd inevitable!——With my babe
I ran defpairing to a lofty tow'r;

       Refolv'd

Refolv'd at once to end our mifery!
Heav'n had not fo decreed!——Preferv'd for
    this!——

ETHA.

Say, how preferv'd?

EMMA.

      A faithful maid withheld me.
She told me that there ftill were hopes of
    life.——
Under the ground the caftle's fountain fent
Into the river its fuperfluous waters.
By that dark winding channel one might pafs
The caftle's limits. On our knees and hands,
Groping our fearful way, at laft we gain'd
Its fartheft end. But there a fteep, rough rock
We muft defcend to reach the river's verge.
I went down firft, and as the maid bent for-
    ward
To give the infant to my outftretch'd arms,
The brittle rock gave way.——She fell, fhe
    died!

ETHA.

ETHA.

But ftill the child was fafe?

EMMA.

A moment's joy
Sooth'd grief and terror to find him unhurt!
But ev'ry object round us threat'ned then
An inftant death; and not lefs horrible.
Aloft the fpiry flames afcend! The ftars
Are in the luftre loft! Far round, the plain
Was vifible as in the light of day.
Clofe by me I beheld unnumber'd ruffians,
Whofe weapons, flafhing through the night,
   fent back
A difmal gleam on their grim vifages!
In thofe I read the features of dire murder,
Intent to make a prey of any wretch,
That might attempt to fly the dreadful
   flames.——
'Twas thou, almighty Pow'r! that gav'ft me
   ftrength!
'Twas thou fupported'ft me and mad'ft me
   fee

The

The friendly fhades along the river's banks
Caus'd by a range of rocks!—Through thofe
    I ftole,
And, unmolefted, reach'd this Druid's cave.
I bleft the kind retreat!——I knew not then
That forrows, ftill more horrid than the paft,
Should thence arife to me, and to my Ofrick!

ETHA.

Ofrick thy fon?

EMMA.

Mine and Cadwallan's too!

ETHA.

From thy mifconduct come thy prefent
    forrows!
Four years are paft fince Britain's King re-
    turn'd,
And yet he knows not of his fon or thee.

EMMA.

Ha! Did you know before of his return?
                   And

And wherefore did you never tell it me?
T' avoid fufpicion I, indeed, declin'd
All talking of him; and I never heard
Of his return, but with the dreadful tale,
Which made me thus fo frantic, thus to rave,
And thus to conjure thee to follow me,
And thus refolv'd to go and tell him all.

ETHA.

But wherefore, fince you chofe me for your
    friend,
Did you conceal yourfelf fo long from me?

EMMA.

Thence all my forrows come!—But in a
    dream,
While here I refted, one, I thought, from
    heav'n,
Bid me with care conceal my fon's defcent;
For when he knew his parents, he fhould
    die,
Fearful I wak'd, and by a dreadful oath
I fwore my ftory never fhould be told.
(Oh! hard neceffity, that now compells me!)

I

I bound the Druid by a fimilar vow
To eternal filence.

ETHA.

Impious 'tis to enquire,
And vain to know the future will of heav'n!
Sorrow foreknown is felt before it comes.
Our blind endeavours to prevent it, oft
Promote it moft.

EMMA.

Too true thy words!—My caution
Brings forth the woes I fear'd!

ETHA.

Is this the Druid?

SCENE

S C E N E VII.

To them the Druid from his cave.

EMMA.

COULD nature hold fo long ?——Art thou
   the fame ?——
The fame thou art, by twenty years un-
   chang'd !

DRUID.

To me all-wafting time had done his worft,
Ere thou didft fee me, Lady ! But though
   thou
Waft then in new-blown beauty's brighteft
   bloom,
That bloom is not fo faded yet by years,
But ftill the princely features I difcern
Of one, whofe prefence honour'd once my
   cell.

Y

EMMA.

EMMA.

I find thou know'ft me!——Druid, doft
thou know
What forrows have from our mifconduct
fprung?

DRUID.

Too well, too well!——The King of Britons now
Was with me here; and Ofrick fcarce had left
me,
When he arriv'd.

EMMA.

Ah!—Whither are they gone?

DRUID.

They go refolv'd each other to deftroy
In fingle combat.

EMMA.

Single combat?—Heav'ns!
Are

Are the moſt horrid means ſelected ſtill
For our undoing?——Guide me to them,
    Druid!

DRUID.

I will, as faſt as theſe my feeble limbs
Can reach the place.

EMMA.

Didſt thou not let them know
The horror that is in this purpos'd combat?

DRUID.

You know I ſwore eternal ſecrecy!

EMMA.

Then all is loſt!——The dreadful deed is
    done!
And now, perhaps, expiring in his wounds,
Panting and pale he lies, whom fav'ring
    heav'n
From greater horror reſcues!—Let me cloſe
His dying eyes!—But ſmile not at his fall,

       Victor

Victor accurs'd!——Soon fhalt thou envy
    him:
Soon blafted fhall thy wreaths of triumph
    be;
And chang'd thy joy to bitternefs and hor-
    ror.

                         [*Exeunt.*

END OF THE THIRD ACT.

ACT

A C T IV.

S C E N E I.

The Outfide of the Wood.

OSRICK, LENA, ELFRIDA, AND HANNA.

OSRICK.

No! thy too anxious fpirit could not bear
Its own emotions at a fight fo fhocking !———
'Twere better to remain within thy tent.
Swift meffengers fhall ev'ry minute fly
To thee with tidings of thy Ofrick's fate:
And thither will I hafte, if I fhall conquer,
To crown my conqueft with my Lena's joy.

LENA.

If you fhall conquer?———Still you fet before me
Uncertain

Uncertain Fortune only in her fmiles!
But fhould it be my Ofrick's fate to fall,
While I'm remov'd, what care fhall ftop his
    wounds?
On what rough pillow fhall his fainting head
Be laid, when Lena's bofom is not nigh?
Shalt thou expire, and fhall I not receive
One poor embrace before I follow thee?

OSRICK.

Confide in heav'n, and banifh ev'ry fear.
Though young, this arm in ftrength or active
    fkill
Is not deficient.——In my breaft I feel
A peaceful confidence, as if my foul
Forefaw th' event fuccefsful as our wifhes.
If I'm deceiv'd,—forget me, O my Lena!—
Blefs thou fome happier prince;—ftill blefs
    the world;
And let thy race long fill Northumbria's
    throne.

LENA.

Live without Ofrick?——What a group of
    horrors

My

My fancy fees in that diftracting thought !
The haughty victor claims me as his due;
By conqueft won !——My race !——Cadwal-
lan's race !——

OSRICK.

No! To fecure thee from fuch fears, a troop,
Selected from our fwifteft cavalry,
Shall ready-mounted wait around thy tent.
They, if I fall in fight, fhall lodge thee fafe
Within the walls of fome bleft fanctuary.

LENA.

Then that bleft fanctuary will be thy
grave !

ELFRIDA.

Near thy own caftle is that famous convent,
To which ill-fated ladies, far and near
Reforting, fly from worldly care and forrow.
As fpring's foft dews and gentle funs reftore
To life the froft-flain beauties of the year,
Devotion there makes minds deprefs'd with
woe

To

To ſmile again in all the bloom of joy.
Thither I'll likewiſe fly, and ſtay with thee.
That ſacred place no ruffian dares invade,
However great or powerful.——Ev'ry Chri-
    ſtian
Would riſe t' avenge ſuch daring ſacrilege.

LENA.

Could I live any where without my Oſrick,
'Twould be in ſuch a ſad ſociety.
With ſympathizing heart I'd hear them all
Relate their various tales of miſery.
But oh! their woes could never equal mine!

OSRICK.

Let not my Lena's fears anticipate
That ſorrow which may never come.——Be
    happy
While yet you may!——Grief ever comes
    too ſoon.——
Our trumpets ſound!—The army all pre-
    par'd!——
Farewell, my Lena!——Thou, her gen'rous
    friend,
                              Farewell

Farewell a while! I hope to meet you foon
In peace and fafety. O, my Queen! farewell!

[*Exit*,

SCENE II.

LENA *(fainting.)*

O MY Ofrick!

ELFRIDA.

Help, Hanna, help, fupport her!

HANNA.

She recovers.

LENA.

Why wilt thou leave me ?——Stop, O ftop
his wounds!
Traitors, ye might have fav'd !——Where am
I ?—Ha!

Z   ELFRIDA,

ELFRIDA.

Lady, there is no frightful object near us.
Thy Ofrick ftill is fafe.

LENA.

My brain's confus'd !———
A fudden damp came o'er my fearful foul,
Prefaging that I ne'er fhould fee him more.
Farewell I would have faid; but on my tongue
The accents fail'd unform'd, and fenfe for-
    fook me.

ELFRIDA.

Ha! 'tis Cadwallan comes !

LENA.

Where fhall we fhun
The hated fight of him ?

ELFRIDA.

Here are fome bufhes.
In thefe we will conceal us, till he pafs.
                    [*They retire.*
                    SCENE

SCENE III.

Enter Cadwallan and Druid.

CADWALLAN.

O WERE this truth !——How fooliſh ! how romantic
Is it to wiſh for what I cannot hope !
Wouldſt thou deceive me? Or art thou deceiv'd?
Both wiſe and honeſt thou waſt ever thought !——
Some dream abſurd it is of doating age !——

DRUID.

Nay then, behold herſelf !

SCENE

SCENE IV.

To them Emma and Randa.

CADWALLAN.

HA! Can it be?
Yet art thou not fome unfubftantial form
Rais'd by fome demon? Emma! Doft thou
     live?

EMMA.

Ah! Canft thou doubt I live, and am thy
     Emma?

CADWALLAN.

Whate'er thou art, I muft embrace thee!——
     Oh!——
My Queen! my Queen!

EMMA.

Thy ever loving wife!

CAD~

Where haft thou been? How, how, didft
    thou efcape
The fire? Ah! wherefore haft thou fhunn'd
    fo long
My kind embraces?——

EMMA.

'Twere tedious now to tell how I efcap'd,
And fince unknown liv'd in Northumbria's
    convent.——
'Till now I never heard of thy return!

CADWALLAN.

Grow, grow forever to my happy heart!
Art thou indeed my Emma?——Stand a-
    part!
Let me again behold thy face!—The fame!—
Oh happinefs beyond my fondeft wifhes!——
The day that brought thee firft a yielding
    bride,
In all the bloom of beauty to my arms,
Gave not fuch blifs as this more happy day,
                     In

In which I find thee now redeem'd from
    death.

EMMA.

O never may a thought of what is paſt
With pain embitter future happineſs.

CADWALLAN.

Torment not thy dear breaſt with what is
        paſt!—
I ne'er forgot thee!—No!——Could I have
        hop'd
To ſee thee thus, my heart had never known
Another flame!—Heav'n knows what pain I
        felt
At my return, to find that thou waſt gone!
'Twas the remembrance of the dear, dear bliſs
I knew with Emma, made me hope to find
Again ſuch pleaſure with another bride :
But in the ſofteſt raptures of that love,
The thoughts of thee ſtill check'd my riſing
        joy,
And tears of ſecret anguiſh flow'd within

EMMA.

EMMA.

I can believe thee, and forgive thee too.
But oh!——My fon!——My fon!——

CADWALLAN.

Thy fon!——Alas! he perifh'd in the
    flames!——
Or was he fav'd?—And did he lately die?
And mourn'ft thou now for him?

EMMA.

       For him and thee!

CADWALLAN.

'Tis impious now to mourn!—Blefs boun-
    teous heav'n,
That thus hath rais'd us, as from death, to
    tafte
Such unexpected, long-defpair'd-of joy!
Nay heav'n in mercy drew this vail of forrow,
O'er th' elfe too dazzling brightnefs of our
    blifs:

                  For

For had our son surviv'd, we must have sunk
Under excess of pleasure.

EMMA.

He survives!

CADWALLAN.

Ha!——Have I heard thee right!

EMMA.

Thy son lives still.

CADWALLAN.

He lives! Where is he? Let me fly t' em-
brace
My son yet never seen! My Emma's son!
He too preserv'd?——Oh happiness too great.

EMMA, (aside.)

Oh happiness too soon I fear to end!

CADWALLAN.

Thy cheeks are wet; but 'tis not with the
streams

Of

Of blifs exftatic as Cadwallan's are!
Thy tears, my Emma, feem with pain to
    flow
From forrow's fountain.

EMMA.
       O my fon! my fon!

CADWALLAN.

His ftate unknown, ferves he the furly
    pride
Of fome poor upftart Lord, to greatnefs grown
Upon the ruins of his rifled fortunes?

EMMA.
O my Cadwallan!—fhun this horrid com-
    bat!
Thy foe thou know'ft not!

CADWALLAN.

       Ofrick's race unknown!
Defend me from fuch thoughts, ye gracious
    Pow'rs!——
Perhaps!——Moft horrid!——

       A a   EMMA.

EMMA.

Ofrick is thy fon!

CADWALLAN.

Ofrick!——Great God!——

(*Whilft he ftands aftonifhed, Lena from the grove, Elfrida holding her.*)

LENA.

Art thou my friend? And wilt thou hold
    me ftill?
To rocks, to floods unfathom'd let my fly!
            [*Exit with Elfrida.*

CADWALALN.

What have I done!——Earth, doft thou
    bear me ftill?
Open thy hollow graves!——Gape from thy
    center!
Difclofe thy yawning womb to fwallow quick
The wretch who never more can face the light!

EMMA,

EMMA.

Wilt thou, for valour once so fam'd, now
 fly
For refuge, like a coward, to despair?

CADWALLAN, *(starting up.)*

Yes!——'Tis a coward's part to wish for
 death!——
Death sits on any sword.

     [*Draws his sword.*

EMMA.

     My Lord!—My life!
What wilt thou do?——By all the tender love
You once profest for Emma——

CADWALLAN.

      Off! Away!
Thou art my bane! my curse! the first dire
 cause
Of all my woe! Accurs'd be that sad day
In which I first beheld thy fatal charms!

    A a 2   EMMA.

EMMA.

Strike here!—O ftrike this breaft belov'd
no more!

CADWALLAN.

Ha! Strike my Emma?——Never, Emma,
never!

EMMA.

Shall Emma live to be thy bane and curfe?
No!——Let me die!——But kill me with the
fword;
And not with fharper curfes and unkindnefs.

CADWALLAN.

Unkindnefs, Emma? I unkind to thee?—
I curs'd, indeed, our fate!——Had I not
caufe?
Have I not caufe for madnefs and defpair?
But thee, for whom my youthful heart firft
felt
The pleafing flames of love, thee, whofe dear
image
                                        Came

Came ev'ry night to foothe me in my dreams,
And feem'd before me all the tedious day;
How may tedious days! while ftormy feas
Kept us afunder; thee, my beft belov'd,
I could not curfe. Yet, yet, we might be
  blefs'd,
Did not thefe hideous monfters of my guilt—

EMMA.

I was th' unhappy caufe!——Be mine the
  guilt!
To him fhew mercy, Heav'n!

CADWALLAN.

    Know'ft thou my crimes?
In heav'n itfelf my foul could tafte no peace.
I carry hell within me!

EMMA.

     Let us hope,
That the difcovery of fome hidden truth
May, by Heav'ns favour, yet reftore our
  peace.

CAD-

CADWALLAN.

Could Heav'n difcover that he's not my fon!
Or Lena not his wife!——I've hear'd, or
    dream'd,
Of fpirits, that have from the cradle ftolen
The rich man's heir, and to his place con-
    vey'd
An infant of fome poor, but virtuous parents,
To be Heav'n's favourite.

EMMA.

        Infants have been chang'd.
Oh! truft to any thing but rafh defpair!

CADWALLAN.

O would to God I could but be deceiv'd!
Tell me how it might be, and I'll compel
My faith, againft all reafon, to believe it,
And ftill purfue him with a rival's rage.

EMMA.

What rival?——O Cadwallan!——Think
    what rival!

CAD-

CADWALLAN.

Have we no caufe to think he was ex-
    chang'd ?

EMMA.

No caufe alas !—Thefe arms through foes
    and fires
To fafety ftole him !——In this Druid's cave
I refted with him. There fallacious dreams
Deceiv'd me. One, I thought from heav'n,
Bid me with care conceal myfelf and him ;
For when he knew his parents he fhould die.

CADWALLAN.

And was it for a dream he was conceal'd?
Thus 'tis to truft the prophecies of hell!
Cadwallan's fon fhould have been known to
    all ;
And ere his manhood led confederate kings
Againft his father's foes, repair'd my palace,
And fhar'd his power with thee : Then had I
    found,
When I return'd, a paradife at home,
                  Inftead

Inftead of ruins, horrors, guilt, and hell.
How was he carried to Northumbria's court?
Didft thou exchange him, Druid?—Say thou
    didft!
I'll give thee half his kingdom.

ÉMMA.

            'Twas not he !——
O'er fteep rough hills, wide valleys, woods
    and rivers
I travell'd with my infant all alone.——
Far to the weft the full-orb'd moon declin'd
The tenth night ere I reach'd to Edwin's gate.
With tears, with prayers, in bleffings and
    embraces,
Till th' envious lark hail'd the returning
    dawn,
I fondly hugg'd him.——Then, good heav'n,
    I left
My dear, dear child to changeful fortune's
    care.

CADWALLAN.

But what determin'd thee to go to Edwin,
                       Not

Not to thy brother Kenwal.

EMMA.

            'Twas my dream,
Determin'd me to travel with my fon
Where neither could be known; and let the
    world
Believe that both had perifh'd in the flames.
Northumbria's famous convent promifed
A dwelling to my wifh; and having heard
Of Edwin's fam'd benevolence, I hop'd
My fon in that might find a father's care.
In that a father's care and more he found.—
Ah! ill-repaid at laft.———

CADWALLAN, (afide.)

           By my curfs'd hand.
That, like a dagger, ftabs me to the heart!

EMMA.

Although a foundling of a race unknown,
He grew in favour, fame, and happinefs,
Till in an evil hour———

                     CAD-

CADWALLAN.

Till that black hour,
In which his father kill'd his better father!
And——Were ye all afleep, ye minifters
Of heav'nly vengeance?——O what mercy
 then
Had been your thunder !——Is his race un-
 known ?

EMMA.

It is unknown to all, but thefe now prefent.

CADWALLAN.

So muft it be for ever ! Could I think
That any here would utter it, my fword
This inftant fhould prevent it.—Yes, the devil
Has once fpoke truth ?——For fure 'twould
 break his heart
To know himfelf the fon of fuch a monfter.
But he fhall never know it.—All muft
 fwear.—
Lay all your hands upon your hearts, and
 fwear,

By

By all your hopes of blifs, and fears of pain,
Here or hereafter, you will ne'er reveal it.

ALL, (*with their hands on their breafts.*)

By all our hopes of blifs and fears of pain,
Here, or hereafter, we will ne'er reveal it.

CADWALLAN.

Then he may live, and in my death be happy.

EMMA.

What means this language?

CADWALLAN.

'Tis refolv'd.

EMMA.

Thy death!

CADWALLAN.

What is beyond the grave?—A long dark chaos

B b 2

Which

Which human fight could never penetrate!
'Twas Superftition firft begot on Fancy
Thofe phantoms which invade our infant
      thoughts,
Ere reafon guards them!—Yet, I find, they
      grow
To a force too great for reafon, or for wifdom,
Or proud philofophy t' expel. Our vanity
In boafting would difguife the weak belief:
But all are confcious of their inward fears!
Ev'n virtue trembles at th' approach of death!
Then what muft guilt, what muft Cadwallan
      feel?

EMMA.

Defpair and horror are in all thy words.

CADWALLAN.

Is it to fall afleep, and wake no more?
Or fhall we, as religion teacheth us,
When thefe our limbs are moulder'd into
      earth,
Exift, and ftill be blefs'd or miferable,
According as our lives have merited!

                O

O God! thou know'ft my life!—But this!—
  O this!——
Could any action for this guilt atone?

EMMA.

Thou haft been more unfortunate than
  guilty,

CADWALLAN.

Yes: There a ray of hope begins to rife,
And in it death's moft dreadful phantoms
  fade!——
Heav'n muft approve, and all its hoft admire
My lateft act!—I die that he may live!——
One laft embrace! And then,—we part for
  ever!

                              [*Going.*

EMMA.

O let me follow thee!

CADWALLAN.

                    I charge thee not.
                              Keep

Keep our important ſecret! Come not near me
Till I am——ſtretch'd in death.

[*Exit,*

SCENE V.

EMMA, ETHA, DRUID,

EMMA.

AND is he gone,
To ruſh upon the weapon of his ſon?
I will prevent it yet!——I'll go to Kenwal;
I'll tell my brother all!——

DRUID.

Have we not ſworn?

EMMA.

Sure perjury were far leſs damnable!
O dreadful oath!——Sworn that we would
permit
The ſon to ſlay the father?

SCENE

SCENE VI.

*(To them enter Lena disordered, Elfrida fol-
lowing.)*

LENA.

SON and father!
If knowingly, and with confenting heart,
Thou haft committed——No. Thou mayft
    repent!
Repent in time! Repent.

ELFRIDA.

Help me to hold her!
It is Northumbria's Queen, driv'n by her
    wrongs
To rave thus wildly.

LENA.

Would'ft thou wrong me too,
Thou with the hoary beard? O beaftly vice!
Deteftable in all; but in the head,

That

That shakes the snow of years, most odious.
  Foh !
Go say thy pray'rs !

EMMA.

She's raving mad !—To me that state were
  bliss !

       [*Exit with Etha.*

S C E N E   VII.

LENA, ELFRIDA, DRUID.

LENA.

THOUGH I by force was to the altar dragg'd
And sacrific'd to devils, I am spotless.
Spotless as thou, or thou !——Ha !—Who
  art thou ?

ELFRIDA.

Dost thou not know me, Lady ?

       LENA.

LENA.

Thee I know,

Thou kindeſt-hearted maid!—When I'm an
 angel,
I'll hover round.——O hadſt thou been an
 angel!
But what is he, who wears that long gray
 beard,
Scoffing old age? Thou art the devil's prieſt?
And would'ſt thou turn me from the way to
 heav'n?
In ſpite of hell, my innocence ſhall ſoar
Above the eagle.——Aye beyond the ſun!

DRUID.

Conduct her to her tent. I'll ſend ſome
 herbs,
Which ſtill the ſenſes to repoſe, and oft
Shake ſuch diſorders from the troubled mind.

LENA.

Who, who ſhall hold me?—See the clouds
 make way

C c

For

For me to enter! Glorious, glorious fight!
Thoufands of angels call me in fweet fongs!
How fhall I to their heav'nly harmony
Attune my mortal voice?

(*Sings.*)

Adieu, vain world of childifh cares!
  Of idle hopes, and foolifh fears!
    Now, now, I take a noble flight,
  Beyond where ftorms and thunders war;
  Beyond each cloud, and ev'ry ftar,
    To th' utmoft bounds of heav'nly light!

ELFRIDA.

Ah! Lady!——Thou may'ft ftill be bleft
  on earth.

LENA.

What! ftill on earth?——Still with a bo-
  dy clogg'd,
That fcents pollution! Off mortality!
Off, off corruption!——
                                [*Tearing her cloaths.*
                                            But

But who fhall guide me through the long,
    dark region
That lies betwixt us and the heav'nly man-
    fions ?——
He comes!—He comes!——Do I not know
    my father?
I faw thy wounds!——I faw thy bofom
    pierc'd !——
I faw thy foul come forth !—Ha! wilt thou
    leave me ?
Stay! wrap me with thee in thy bloody
    fhroud!

        [*Runs out,* *they all follow her.*

END OF THE FOURTH ACT.

        A C T

A C T V.

S C E N E I.

AN OPEN PLAIN.

Prince Arthur, with some officers of the Britons.

ARTHUR.

Before thou sett'st, O sun, thou may'st be-
    hold
Thy rays flash from a crown on Arthur's
    brow.

FIRST OFFICER.

  Yes, valiant Arthur, if Cadwallan fall,
Thou art the first in merit as in blood
To rule the antient Britons.

SECOND

SECOND OFFICER.

              'Tis reported,
That the conditions of the fight will be,
That he who conquers fhall poffefs the realm
Of him that falls.

ARTHUR.

         No !—While the ftreams of life
Run in my veins, though Britons all forfake
    me,
I will oppofe it with my fingle fword.
I'll be your King, or die attempting it.

ALL THE OFFICERS.

We with our lives will Arthur's right
    maintain.

ARTHUR.

So ev'ry Briton fhould.——But Britons
    now
No longer breathe that free, that manly fpi-
    rit,

                       With

With which our fires untaught, unarm'd, oppos'd
Th' all conquering Romans. Ev'n our women then,
Fierce in the front of war, perform'd such
   feats,
As their enfeebled fons now quake to hear.

THIRD OFFICER.

Both combatants now to this fpot advance;
Whence one of them muft never more depart.

SECOND OFFICER.

Our King approaches.

ARTHUR.

   If my judgement err not,
There is a ftrange confufion in his looks!
       [*They go to a fide.*

SCENE

SCENE II.

Enter Cadwallan.

(A trumpet heard.)

CADWALLAN.

THE trumpet and the impending war no
    more
Excite the raptures they were wont to do!
Now, like the death-man's warning to the fe-
    lon,
They fummon me to my determin'd doom!
Hence ev'ry fear?——Rife valour's wonted
    flame,
Rife, royal pride, and fentiments of honour,
Rife in my breaft!——Let me with dignity
And kingly grace conclude a life of troubles!

SCENE

SCENE III.

*Enter Kenwal with his attendants, and Osrick
with his.*

KENWAL.

Y E Princes, range yourfelves in order round.

*(Ofrick and his nobles arrange themfelves on the
fide of the ftage oppofite to Cadwallan and his.
Kenwal draws up his officers, with guards,
on the front and back part between them.)*

KENWAL.

The combat now proceeds, if all approve.

CADWALLAN.

I do approve.

OSRICK.

And I.

ALL

ALL THE OFFICERS.

And all of us.

KENWAL.

Then Britifh and Northumbrian chiefs,
    give ear,
To the conditions which I've fworn to en-
    force.——
If any dare infringe them, or difturb,
By weapon, action, gefture, fignal, word,
Or any other way; the combatants,
I join the other fide, againft th' aggreffor,
With my whole force.——Whatever Prince's
    fate
It is to fall, both armies muft difperfe,
And with revengeful wars on this account
Exhauft no more the precious blood of Albion,

CADWALLAN.

More muft be added.—Let the conquering
    King
Inherit the dominions of the vanquifh'd;

           And

And the fair prize for which the war began,
Northumbria's Queen, become the victor's
    due.

OSRICK.

From this I muſt diſſent.—Northumbria's
    Queen,
Or her dominions, nothing can transfer
But her own free conſent.

CADWALLAN.

                    With that alone
I wiſh to have her.   Be my kingdom thine,
If I ſhould fall.—And I, through Lena's love,
If 'tis thy fate, expect to inherit thine.

OSRICK.

Through Lena's love !—To the moſt odious
    monſter
That crawls on earth ſhe'd fly t' avoid thy
    love!

CADWALLAN, (aſide.)

O ſcorn that well becomes thee! Yet forbear,
                                    My

My fwelling heart, elfe I muft lofe my pur-
    pofe.
Oh that I now could clafp thee to my breaft!
But that muft never be!——Come on, thou
    braggart!

OSRICK.

Aye! to thy heart thou monfter!——Ha!
what now?

S C E N E IV.

AN OLD SOLDIER, (*entering haftily.*)

Emma!——The tale fo much exceeds be-
    lief,
That, mighty Princes, though thefe eyes have
    feen her,
I fhould be dumb, were fhe not here herfelf
To vouch it.

KENWAL.

Emma!—Who!—What Emma doft
    thou mean?
                    D d 2   SOLDIER.

SOLDIER.

Emma, thy fister! The fair Queen of Britons!
Like one diftracted with her fears fhe raves!
The foldiers cannot, without violence,
Withhold her from her hufband.

KENWAL.

And knew you this?

CADWALLAN.

Ah! let her not difturb the combat now.—
But, if I fall, O Kenwal, comfort Emma!—
Now, Ofrick, come.

OSRICK.

For Lená and her wrongs.
                    [*Fight.*

(*As they are fighting, Emma comes behind the
attendants of Kenwal.*)

KENWAL.

Amazing providence!—'Tis fhe, indeed!
                    SCENE

SCENE V.

EMMA.

YE traitors! murderers!——Let me fave
    his life!
My brother! Canft thou calmly ftand to fee
A fight fo fhocking?

KENWAL, *(holding her.)*

Emma!——My fifter!——For the love of
    heav'n!——
You give th' advantage to his enemy!——

EMMA.

You know not what you do!——He falls!
    He's flain!

CADWALLAN, *(falling.)*

Aye, juftly flain!——The better caufe
    prevails!

                           [Dies.

                      EMMA.

EMMA.

And art thou gone !———Thou canſt return
  no more !
O my Cadwallan ! O my love ! My huſband !
                    [*Falling on the body.*

OSRICK.

Haſte Anfrid, tell the Queen of our ſucceſs!
Tell her, that I by this revenge have gain'd
The kingdom of the Briton. Let our trumpets
Proclaim our victory to all around.

    [*Northumbrian trumpets found, and the ar-
      my ſhouts within.*

ARTHUR, (*coming forward.*)

Kenwal, you know my claim to Britain's
  throne !
And you, who would uſurp that diadem,
Which never ſat but on a Briton's brow,
Know, that ſince this brave Prince's hapleſs fall,
I am the firſt of that illuſtrious blood
Which govern'd Britons ſince their race be-
  gan.
Nor can Cadwallan's will rob me of that
                              Which

Which cuftoms, antient and invariable
As Albion's mountains, have confirmed mine.

OSRICK.

Yourfelf and all agreed to the conditions.
'Tis mine by conqueft;—and it fhall remain
 fo!

ARTHUR.

It is not conquer'd while one Briton lives.

KENWAL.

By thefe old cuftoms you have mention'd,
 Emma
May claim the crown; for Britons ever fuffer'd
The Queen of him who rul'd them laft, to
 reign
During her life.——My fifter, then, arife,
And claim thy kingdom!——Leave a breath-
 lefs hufband!
A brother ftill is here to guard. thy right.

EMMA, (*rifing.*)

My brother! Oh! in any hour but this
         Of

Of hopelefs mifery, that fight were happinefs!

KENWAL.

Alas! What miferies has Emma fuffer'd!
O my poor fifter!—I muft mourn with thee.

OSRICK, (*afide.*)

Her anguifh wrings my heart! Revenge is
dead!
She never did me wrong.—But why fhould I
Feel thus the forrows of an enemy?

EMMA, (*afide looking on Ofrick.*)

Didft thou bring all thefe miferies on me?
Thou dear unhappy boy! But down my heart.

ARTHUR, (*afide.*)

She looks not on the man that flew her
Lord
With ftern, refentment, or with hatred's
frown!——
Nay, there is fomething more.—By heav'ns,
affection!

EMMA.

How could you permit it?————
How could you, O my brother, fee him flain?

KENWAL.

Ha! Did Cadwallan know thou waft in
    life?
Did he forget thee, then, in the conditions,
Which he propos'd himfelf? Yes, while thou
    liv'ft,
Thou fhalt, my fifter, be the Queen of Bri-
    tons.

EMMA.

No earthly kingdom now can give me
    joy!
Cadwallan's will be done in ev'ry thing.

ARTHUR.

Hear this, ye Britons!—Now, with man-
    ly hearts
Repel this fhame; or hide your daftard heads
With hunted monfters in the barren rocks,

To which ufurping Saxons have confin'd you.
Shall Britain's throne, that never yet was
    fill'd,
But by a race defcended from the gods,
Be now polluted by——we know not whom?
A baftard of fome namelefs flave, produc'd
By fome lewd dame; who, that fhe might
    . again
Purfue without reftraint her fordid pleafures,
Expos'd her child to ftarve ;—or feed on alms?

OSRICK.

Ruffian! no more.——

EMMA.

           Ungenerous and unjuft!
Wherefore afperfe th'unknown with foul con-
    jectures?
Perhaps his mother, virtuous, chaft as thine,
Nor lefs illuftrious——

ARTHUR.

        You efpoufe his caufe!
Perhaps his mother from her hufband ftaid

                  To

To wanton in fome younger lover's arms!
Perhaps fhe had put on religion's vail,
And, to maintain her fanctity, was forc'd
To difavow her child of many fathers.
Such ladies we have heard of:—Such we've
    feen!
But fhall the fon of fuch be King of Britons?

ALL THE BRITISH OFFICERS.

We with our lives will Arthur's right defend.

NORTHUMBRIAN OFFICERS.

And we brave Ofrick's.

OSRICK.

        Let the King of Weffex,
Let the Northumbrian and the Britifh chiefs
Be witneffes of yet another combat.——
Upon this fland'rous ruffian I'll refent
My unknown mother's wrongs; affert my
    right
To this new fceptre which my arm has won,
Or perifh in th' attempt.

EMMA.

EMMA.

Hold, forward youth!
Endanger not thy life!—'Tis juftly thine!—

KENWAL.

How, Emma! What means this?

EMMA.

What have I done!

ETHA. (*afide.*)

Refiftlefs force of nature!

ARTHUR.

Shamelefs woman!
Widow'd this moment, and in love the next!
Why this is rank indeed!——You might be mother
To that bafe youth on whom your paffion dotes.

EMMA.

All-gracious Heav'n!

ARTHUR.

ARTHUR.

Why do you ftart at this?
But ha !—'Tis poffible your artful brain
May rear a fine romance to raife your fav'rite.
Cadwallan had a fon: Swear this is he!
That angels fnatch'd him from the flames,
    and flew
O'er cruel foes to Edwin's court with him.

KENWAL.

Cadwallan's fon had been of Ofrick's age!
Say what, my fifter was the fate of him?
Did he efcape with you from flames and foes?

EMMA.

Whate'er his fate, my mifery's compleat!

OSRICK.

" Efcape from flames and foes !"—So fpake
    the Druid.
To a kingdom I was born, he likewife faid.
'Twas in this kingdom !——Every myftery
                Appears

Appears moft plain!——He fought not with
    the art
Of fo renown'd a warrior:—Yet I flew him.
Great God! I flew the author of my birth!

EMMA.

His words are madnefs!——Bear ye hence,
    my friends,
Thefe dear remains to fome fequefter'd grove;
There with my tears I'll wafh thy bloody
    wounds,
O my Cadwallan!—My unhappy hufband!
      [*They are going to carry off the body.*

OSRICK.

No!—Let me fall upon my murder'd fa-
    ther!——
Let tears of penitence wafh out this ftain!
O Lady, pity me!

EMMA.

Ha!——Pity thee?

OSRICK.

Forgive me! Pity me!——O curfe me not!
               EMMA.

EMMA.

Ohaſte, my Etha, bear me from his preſence.

OSRICK.

Ah leave me not in this perplexity!
I feel thy ſorrows!—They are all my own!

EMMA.

Wherefore, O wherefore am I forc'd to
this?

OSRICK.

Forc'd! to reſtrain th' affection of a mother?
In my embraces let it copious flow.

EMMA.

Embraces!—Murderer of my huſband!—
thine?

OSRICK.

Harſh are thy words! Yet through the
rough reproach,
I thought I heard affection's ſoften'd tone.—
The

The fweets of filial love I never felt:
But fure they're wondrous like what now I
 feel.
At the firft fight of thee my bofom heav'd!
My fympathifing heart leapt towards thine!
My fpirits ftarted to their utmoft bounds,
Approving, though I thought thee then my
 foe!

EMMA.

'Twas a delufion wild!

OSRICK, (*kneeling.*)

The happy raptures, when a parent prays
For bleffings on the offspring of his love,
I never knew.——O let me know them now

EMMA.

My bleffing!

OSRICK.

  No! I have deferv'd thy curfe!
Thy bittereftcurfe!—Yes. Curfe the parricide;
Though, haplefs wretch! he knew not of his
 crime.

EMMA.

I will not curfe thee youth; and muft not
blefs thee.

[*Exit with Etha.*

SCENE VI.

OSRICK.

Uncertain ftill!———What think'ft thou,
King of Weffex?

KENWAL.

That fo fhe would behave, were fhe your
mother;
And had fome reafon for diffembling thus.

SCENE

SCENE VII.

Enter Anfrid and Elfrida.

ANFRID.

Mⁱᵍʰᵗ MY King!—My friend!——Alas!——

OSRICK.

Can you not speak?——
Ah! Muft I gueſs it Anfrid!——You have
heard
Of Ofrick's horrid act.—Has Lena heard it?

ANFRID.

Too ſure ſhe has.——Diſtracted ſee ſhe
comes!

S C E N E VIII.

Enter Lena, fupported by Hanna, and the Druid.

LENA.

AYE, wherefore not!——How fhould he know his father?
And fathers may be wicked!—Men are frail,
As well as women.——

OSRICK.

Worfe! O worfe than death!

LENA.

It is the houfe of death! Thefe his attend-
ants!
I know you all!—Your names are on your
faces!
Thou art Remorfe! thou Vengeance! thou
Defpair!

And

And thou lean Envy, with thy curling fnakes!
Why do they roll, and gape, and hifs at me!
I have no heart! Long fince was that con-
　　fum'd
By fnakes more venomous!

OSRICK.

She knows me not!

LENA.

Did Ofrick fpeak? Where is he?

OSRICK.

Here my Lena!

LENA.

Art thou my Ofrick!——No, no, no.——
Sweet rofy health, and youth, and manly
　　courage
Bloom'd in my hero's cheek.——Pale fear's
　　on thine,
And wither'd age and wrinkles!——Save me
　　angels!
It is the Briton!——Haft thou flain my love?
　　　　　　　　　　　　　　　OSRICK.

OSRICK.

O Lena!—O my Queen!

LENA.

Villain! and doft thou glory in the deed?
And doft thou know what blood is on thy
    fword?
It is thy fon's!——
Frown, rage! I care not! Wilt thou kill me?
    ——Do.
For Ofrick was thy fon! He's in my heart,
There kill him o'er again.
Rivet our hearts together.

OSRICK, (*taking hold of her.*)

Ah! Let us take her hence.

LENA.

Villain, unhand me!—Ruffian, let me go!
Kill, kill me twenty times.——But keep
    aloof!——
Wilt thou indeed?——Help, O my Ofrick,
    help me!

                                    O!

Thou parricide! Thou coward!—kill a woman!
O!—I am flain!—Struck to the heart?—Oh
    Death!
Why doft thou grin fo horribly?
Ye hideous fpectres of the rotten graves,
Why do ye fhake your ghaftly heads?——
But Ofrick waits me!——'Tis my father's
    fpirit!——
Take me to heaven.——

                        [*Dies.*

OSRICK.

Is Lena gone? Shall I not follow her?
Why fhould the murderer of a father live?
                [*Drawing his fword.*

KENWAL.

Hold, hold thy defp'rate hand.

                              SCENE

S C E N E IX.

EMMA, (*entering.*)

MY fon! my fon!
Unhappy fon of moft unhappy parents!
What wilt thou do?

OSRICK.

Revenge a father's death.

EMMA.

On me, on me! Revenge his death on me!
I was the caufe of it!

OSRICK.

On thee!——My mother!

EMMA.

Yes.——In my bofom hide thy fword; for
there

'Twill

'Twill give lefs painful, not lefs certain death;
Than 'twould in thine!

OSRICK.

What monfter were I then?
The murderer accurs'd of both my parents!

EMMA.

If you deftroy yourfelf, you murder me!

OSRICK.

I'll rather live in everlafting torture!——
But much I fear, I have not always been
So near thy heart: Elfe wherefore didft thou
     leave me?
Leave me in ignorance, to act fuch horrors?

EMMA.

Horrors indeed! Moft horrible to me?—
But thou art innocent.——He had refolv'd,
Before you met, to die upon thy fword.

OSRICK.

Ha!——Did he know it then?

EMMA.

EMMA.

      A little fpace
Before his death, he heard it from my mouth.
My anxious care and caution to preferve thee
Has brought thy ruin !——O my fon forgive
   me !——
For in a dream I thought that I was told,
By one, whom I believ'd to be from heav'n,
That, when thou knew'ft thy parents thou
   fhould'ft die.

OSRICK.

If 'twas foretold by heav'n, it muft be fo !
What have I now in life ?

EMMA.

     Thou haft a mother !
That has none left but thee to comfort her !
O think what pains, what cares, what fearful
   days,
And fleeplefs nights fhe fuffer'd for thy fake !

   G g   OSRICK,

OSRICK.

Sure fome divinity looks from thine eyes,
Or in thine accents breathes, that charms de-
    fpair!
And ftilling ev'ry tumult of my mind,
Fills all my breaft with reverence and love!
How can I comfort thee?——Command thy
    fon.
I'm all obedience.

EMMA.

                    Caft away that fword,
And wait with patience for the ftroke of
    heav'n.

OSRICK.

Good caufe haft thou to execrate this
    fword!
Yet once on this my youthful fancy rear'd
A tow'ring edifice of future fame,
That fhould outlive the marble monument!——
Stain'd with a father's blood!—Hence from
    my fight!——

                                        Adieu

Adieu forever all a warrior's hopes!
Far diftant from the haunts of bufy men,
With only thee, my mother, will I ftay;
Shed ev'ry day fome tears of fad remem-
  brance,   •
And patient wait for the relief of heav'n'!
'Twill not be tedious, if thy dream deferves
Our confidence!

EMMA.

    O, had it ne'er been trufted!
Too late, by what it has produc'd, we find
It came from hell.———Delufive 'twas and
  falfe!

OSRICK.

  Perhaps 'twas true!———Perhaps equivo-
  cal:
For now, departing from the cares of life,
I to the world may be accounted dead.
Then hear my dying will.———Prince Arthur,
   thou,
For 'tis thy right when I am gone, fhalt
  wear

The Britiſh crown. 'Tis thine, my faithful
    Anfrid,
Since Lena is no more, to wear Northum-
    bria's.
Thou, generous maid of Weſſex, if my
    pray'rs
Had pow'r to effect it, ſhould'ſt be Anfrid's
    Queen.

ANFRID.

I ever lov'd you, as my Prince and friend.
Yet, ſince I knew this Princeſs, I confeſs,
I wiſh'd for thrones of kings or emperors,
To raiſe her equal to her great deſerts.
Yet, thus obtain'd, it yields no pleaſure.—
    Reign,
And let me ſtill be happy in thy friendſhip.

OSRICK.

No.——'Tis reſolv'd?——My only king-
    dom now
Shall be ſome lonely cottage in a deſart.
But what ſay'ſt thou, the brother of my mo-
    ther,

                      Of

Of this propos'd alliance?——Speak your
    thoughts:
And thou, his lovely daughter! ,

KENWAL.

                   Elfrida's eyes
Exprefs confent.   Then take my daughter,
    Anfrid.
And may fhe prove the pledge of lafting
    peace
'Twixt Weffex and Northumbria.——Arthur
    too,
Who art our kinfman; and ye Princes all,
Let us unite like brothers, and defy
The vain attempts of ev'ry foreign foe.

ARTHUR.

With pleafure I agree.

ALL THE CHEFTAINS.

                And all of us.

KENWAL.

May never foul diffention, from the plots
                             Of

Of bafe felf-intereft, or the envious views
Of falfe ambition, turn a Briton's foul
From acting for his country's common good

DRUID.

Your children's children, and their latef
     race
Shall blefs you the firft founders of thi
     union.
For, when this ifland all fhall fo unite,
Old feers foretel, that Britain's pow'r fhal
     ftride
From the fun's rifing to his fetting place.

THE END.

be following tragedy being less correct than any other of the author's writings, it was at first resolved to omit it in the present publication; and, in that view, one of the choruses, and parts of two others were inserted among the smaller poems. The friends of the author, however, have since desired the insertion of the tragedy entire; and they trust to the candour of the public, for their indulgent reception of a piece which never underwent the author's last corrections.

D ARTHULA,

A

TRAGEDY.

Hh

PERSONS.

CAIRBAR, King of *Erin*.
CATHMOR, his Brother.
COLLA, an *Erinian* Nobleman.
DARTHULA, his Daughter.
USNOTH, a *Caledonian* Nobleman.
NATHOS and ARDAN, his Sons.
ALTHAN, the Bard of *Cormac*.
CARRIL, another Bard.
DERMID, a Soldier of *Nathos'* Army.

Guards, Soldiers, &c.

SCENE, *The coaſt of Ullin, or Ulſter, in Ir* land.

A C T I.

SCENE, *Before Colla's Castle.*

Colla and some of his Officers.

COLLA.

THE time's important! Ev'ry moment now
May lead us on to glorious deeds of war:
Our youthful general, eager to revenge
The death of great Cuchullin, and to prop
The tottering throne of Erin's minor King,
Basely attack'd by Atho's cruel Lord,
Promis'd this morn to greet us by the dawn.
Nathos will soon be here. The morning now
Already blushes o'er us. Yon long streams,
Brigh'tning the tremulous ocean, shew where
   soon
The glorious sun shall blaze above the waves.

FIRST OFFICER.

One comes with hafty ftride.

SECOND OFFICER.

It is the General.

NATHOS, (*entering.*)

Hail, worthy Colla!——Are your troops
prepar'd?

COLLA.

The leaders wait you here.

NATHOS.

With inftant fpeed,
Brave warriors, join the right wing of our
front:
For ev'ry moment we expect t' engage.
All elfe is ready.

[*Exeunt officers.*

COLLA.

Have thofe troops return'd,
Who

Who at the brave Cuchullin's fall difpers'd?

NATHOS.

They come with joy, and fay they fee in me
Their former leader.   For it feems, my fea-
    tures
Refemble his.——O for a mind like his!
Whofe bold ambition fpurr'd him on to fame,
By the fure paths which prudent virtue pointed.
Whofe courage fmil'd at danger's threat'ning
    front,
And never yielded to oppofing hardfhips;
But met them like a fea-furrounded rock,
Unmov'd by all the fury of the ftorm.

COLLA.

May Cormac's youth a guardian find in
    thee,
Faithful like him, brave and magnanimous:
But of a better fortune, to repel
Th' ungenerous foes, who now fo bafely
    come
To wreft the fceptre from a ftripling's hand.
Cairbar fhall fail, as all his fathers did

When

When they affail'd the kingdom of the North.

NATHOS.

This tyrant Cairbar is of dreadful fame,
Not for his valour, but his artful frauds
In th' intervals of war ; and cruel deeds,
When by fuccefs his fullen pride is fwell'd.

COLLA.

Then only is he dreadful. In the field
The coward fhrinks from danger.——All his
      frauds
Will by this vigilance in thee be foil'd:
Since, though late watching in the nightly
      cold,
Thou thus canft brave the chilling damps of
      morn.

NATHOS.

In fummer, and in Erin's temperate clime,
Nocturnal coolnefs brings delight to me,
Who hardy grew among the fharper frofts
Of Caledonia's hills.—There with the dawn
Our father led his fons into the woods,
                Where

Where we have chac'd the ſtag till night re-
    priev'd him;
Lain down to reſt beneath a tufted oak,
And with the morning ſtar renew'd our toil.
Theſe exerciſes will, my ſons, ſaid Uſnoth,
Shake from your growing limbs the ruſt of
    ſloth;
They'll temper your young nerves with active
    ſpring,
To ſpeed the jav'lin in more glorious fields,
And bear unhurt th' illuſtrious toil of arms.

COLLA.

Such are the rugged paths that lead to
    fame!
Let youth by hardy labour grow to ſtrength;
And while in vigour do what they may boaſt
    of,
When envious age has left no other joy.
The feebleſt foes now ſhun not my approach,
And cowards ſtand t' inſult my ſhaking arm.
Thy father knows it was not always ſo.
The proudeſt foes have fled from this old arm,
And op'ning ranks before it ſhew'd their fear.

Is

Is Ufnoth's ftrength, like mine, decay'd with
 age.

NATHOS.

Like thee my father feels the weight of
 years;
But ftill his vigour can, like thine, fupport it.

COLLA.

Methinks I fee thy father young again,
Brave fon of Ufnoth, while I look on thee.
The pleafures of our youth rufh on my mind.
Together have we rang'd the favage wilds,
And fide by fide the battle's dangers brav'd!
O in fuch thoughts I could forgot my age,
And tire thee with an old man's tedious ftories,
Of wonders then atchiev'd.——May all thy
 wars,
Like Ufnoth's, be the fav'rite fong of fame.

NATHOS.

In hopes of this our father fent us hither;
Where, while defending Erin's minor king,
Under our warlike uncle, we might learn
       Th'

Th' experienc'd leader's practice.—But alas!
When scarce we had unsheath'd our maiden
    swords,
Cuchullin fell; and I, though small my skill,
And almost ere I wish'd it, by the friends
Of Cormac am elected General.——

COLLA.

Oh happy Usnoth! thou hast sons to wield
Thy weighty weapons!——Ah! had mine
    remain'd!
We now perhaps with pleasure had beheld
    them
Attach'd by warm affection, like their fa-
    thers,
In friendly emulation, rise to fame.

NATHOS.

Favour'd by his coeval Prince, one son,
Fruthil, the youngest, yet remains to bless
    thee,
And rise the Colla of his Cormac's reign.—
Thy daughter too.——Darthula's peerless
    charms

I i

May.

May make the proudeſt Prince become more
      proud,
To hail thee for a father. O how bleſs'd,
Beyond expreſſing bleſs'd, were I to find
You thought me not unworthy of the honour
Of joining, by an everlaſting bond,
The race of Colla with the line of Uſnoth.

COLLA.

Thou art deſerving of the higheſt honours!
When leiſure ſerves I'll tell thee more of this.
Think now upon th' importance of thy charge!
Thouſands confide to thee their lives their
      all!
Darthula comes.——In few words take your
      leave:
For now a moment's chance may be deciſive.
                 [*Exit.*

NATHOS, (alone)

Wiſe is the counſel!——The reproach is
      juſt!
My traitor heart!—Is this a time for love?

                    Enter

Enter Darthula and attendant.

DARTHULA.

Young foldier, I difturb your private
 thoughts!
I break perhaps fome plans of future con-
 queft,
Or great ideas of expected fame.
Such contemplations to the brave, I'm told,
Afford a joy like real victory.

NATHOS.

No joy, no pleafure is to me like this
With which Darthula's prefence fills my
 breaft.
Sweet are the hopes of fame; revenge is fweet
For my dear kinfman flain; but when with
 thee,
Heedlefs of fame, unmindful of revenge,
A gentler paffion gives me fweeter joy.
Oh could I hope that fair Darthula felt
With me fuch pleafure, we fhould never part!
Not ev'n old age fhould leffen our delight,
But turn youth's raptures to a milder joy.

DAR-

DARTHULA.

Of this important time can Nathos lofe
A fingle fecond in fuch idle thoughts?
See danger imminent befets us clofe,
And all to thee, as their defender, look.

NATHOS.

The time's important! But O tell me this,
Before I go :—Forgive an anxious lover!
Have I no rival?——Some brave youth, per-
    haps,
By former feats already crown'd with fame,
Amidft his trophies offer'd you his heart,
Which you regard as no unwelcome prize.

DARTHULA.

You have a rival. You have caufe to fear.

NATHOS.

Have caufe to fear! Darthula fees me trem-
    ble!
But bring this rival bath'd in vanquifh'd
    blood,
                        Frowning

Frowning in fullen pride of victory,

Burning with rage, exulting in his ftrength,

His fword prepar'd, his body fheath'd in
 fteel,

I will not fear him.—Who's this happy rival?

DARTHULA.

Cairbar——

NATHOS.

   The tyrant! He Darthula's love!

Then, fhould good fortune from my happy
 arm

Send death to this deftroyer of mankind,

What will the fruits of my wifh'd conqueft
 be?

Darthula's tears!——No. Reft in peace, my
 fword.

But if I fall beneath the ftrength of Cairbar,

When thou fhalt fee this head upon his
 fpear——

DARTHULA.

O never! never!——Spare the dreadful
 image!——

With

With thee I'll die.——With thee, with thee,
    I'll live!

NATHOS.

Ah! mock me not; for—Cairbar is my
    rival.

DARTHULA.

Cairbar has often importun'd my love:
But him of all mankind I moſt deteſt.

NATHOS.

Didſt thou not ſay, that I had cauſe to fear
    him?

DARTHULA.

More cauſe have I to fear his brutal tem-
    per!
Thinking of that, what horror harrows me!
What if ſome chance of unſucceſsful war
Put me in Cairbar's power?

NATHOS.

    There, there, you paint,
                  In

In ſtrongeſt features, war's worſt miſery.
Shall I, in chains perhaps, behold Darthula
Torn from her Nathos by ſome ruffian's
  force,
And dragg'd away, and us'd unworthily.

DARTHULA.

Why are our fears the ſame? Sure fancy
  ſees,
With eyes prophetic, our impending fate!
Such horrors ever haunt my waking thoughts,
And dreadful viſions paintthem in my dreams.
Did my moſt ardent wiſhes aught avail,
This inſtant war ſhould ſheath his bloody
  ſword,
And Nathos ne'er ſhould ſee the face of dan-
  ger.

NATHOS.

Then Nathos never could deſerve thy love.
     [*Diſtant ſhouts heard.*
The army ſhouts ?——Sweet time-deceiving
  love!
I've ſtaid too long.

        [*Exit.*
       Darthula,

Darthula, and attendant.

DARTHULA.

And bid me not farewell!
Who knows if ever I fhall fee him more?

ATTENDANT.

He goes to fight with as much fearlefs joy,
As the young hunter to his fporting field.

DARTHULA.

With joy!——What joy can war and dan-
 ger yield?
War, the deftruction of the great and brave,
Seems in reflection's eyes a monfter grim,
Befmear'd with blood of kindred lately torn?
Yet men, how ftrange! as if in love with
 horror,
Delighted, rufh before his cruel fangs!
     [*Diftant noife of battle.*
O Love! thou heap'ft new terrors on my
 mind!
I fear'd enough before for Colla's age;
         For

For Fruthil, in the tender bloom of youth;
The hated infolence of Cairbar's love,
And all the common woes that follow war:
For father, brother, country, and myfelf,
I fear not now fo much as for my Nathos.
Ye pow'rs who rule th' uncertain fate of war!
Who from your fav'rites turn the deadly
       fhaft,
And guide deftruction to the deftin'd heart!
This day let Nathos be your foremoft care!
Around his head unfeen your armour fpread,
And near him let no hurtful weapon come!

Enter Colla.

COLLA.

This, my Darthula, is the curfe of age!—
When was a battle in my hearing fought,
And I not active in its hotteft place?
In thought's firft tranfports fometimes I re-
    folve
To rufh, as I had wont, into the ftrife:
But thefe decay'd, old, difobeying limbs
Too foon remind me of my feeble ftate.

        K k   DAR-

DARTHULA.

My father, you have had your fhare of
fame,
And with that fhare may well reft fatisfy'd.
[*Shouts at a diftance.*

COLLA.

Heard you not that?——One of the fides
prevails.

DARTHULA.

Which of the fides?——

COLLA.

Alas! I know not that.
[*More fhouts.*
But thefe are fure the fhouts of victory.

DARTHULA.

The noife approaches us!——Perhaps our
fate!
If Nathos falls or flies!——If Cairbar comes,
Elate with victory, what fhall we do?
COLLA.

COLLA.

His cruelty, indeed, is to be fear'd.

DARTHULA.

Much caufe have we to fear his cruelty!
But more I fear,—much more, his hated love!

COLLA.

O my Darthula! ever hate his love.——
Thou haft been ever dear as life to me;
And yet, methinks, before I faw thee Cair-
   bar's,
I'd fee thee dead!

DARTHULA.

Then dead thou firft fhalt fee me.

COLLA.

Thou fpeak'ft, I fear, and haft not thought
  of death.
Could'ft thou refign the pleafant hopes of joy,
That youth and beauty may expect in life,
Blefs'd with the love of a young hero, form'd
    K k 2   With

With all that foftly charms the heart, or
    fwells
Ambition's wifh.

DARTHULA.

    There's no fuch hope with Cairbar!
Our hopes in life before us often fly,
Delufive as the rainbow's fleeting radiance;
Which fimple boys purfue for fabled trea-
    fure.
If Nathos falls, what hope can flatter me?

COLLA.

Now we fhall hear!—See fome come from
    the battle.

DARTHULA.

Protecting pow'rs! a party ftrong in arms!

COLLA.

The foldiers halt. Forward their leader
    comes!
Sure they are friends!

DAR-

DARTHULA.

Yes. Nathos' brother tis !
Ardan, I know.

COLLA.

What tidings doft thou bring?
How goes the battle?

ARDAN, (*entering.*)

All as yet goes well,
Since there's no battle here. My brother
fear'd
From Cairbar's motions fome new ftrata-
gem;
And, left to feize Darthula be his aim,
Sent us to guard you. By a different rout,
Our brother Athos, with the fwifteft youths,
Was to the royal refidence difpatch'd.

COLLA.

What were the motions that produc'd fuch
fears?

ARDAN.

ARDAN.

At founding of the charge; not half their
    force
Advanc'd into the plain t' attack our front.
Of them we made a fhort and eafy conqueft.
Our fcouts defcry'd a ftronger party move,
Wide from the battle, on our left wing's fide:
Thefe we expected on our flank or rear,
And our referves ftood ready to receive them.
Their way continuing ftill through hollow
    paths,
Their deftin'd purpofe they as yet conceal.

COLLA.

Cairbar's deceitful, grov'ling, coward
    foul,
Which love of fame, or glory, ne'er infpir'd,
Has now in head fome fordid view of intereft,
Or plunder, to be got with little rifk.

DARTHULA.

I fear it is a ftorm of cruelty,
That foon will burft on fome devoted head !
                Should

Should he come hither!

ARDAN.

        Hither let him come,
That I may likewife have my fhare of fame!

DARTHULA.

Ah, youthful warrior!—Thou mayft often
  have
Such opportunities t' acquire renown:
Wifh not for danger to thy early life.

ARDAN.

When valour falls, Fame gives a better life;
A life not mortal by the ftroke of fteel;
A life to bloom in everlafting youth,
When monuments are funk beneath the foil,
And level with the plain yon mountains lie.

DARTHULA.

More warriors from the battle!—Nathos
    comes!
And comes with victory!

ARDAN.

ARDAN.

But who is he,
Yon captive chief of such a goodly mien?

DARTHULA.

Is it the tyrant's brother?

COLLA.

Yes: 'Tis Cathmor.
Generous, humane, and brave, in war or
peace,
Cathmor, for ev'ry virtue is esteem'd,
As much as Cairbar is for crimes detested.

Enter Nathos with Cathmor prisoner.

Guards.—A soldier carrying Cathmor's sword.

NATHOS.

Colla, you see the glorious prize we've made.
The valiant Cathmor!

COLLA.

COLLA.

With a brighter wreath,
Conqueſt ne'er bound the happy victor's
· brow !——
Brave Cathmor, think not that thou here
ſhalt find
A barbarous foe, t'increaſe with cruel inſult,
The bitter galling of a captive's chains.

CATHMOR.

'Tis not captivity that galls me moſt.

NATHOS.

The brave and generous man finds ev'ry
where
Th'eſteem and friendſhip of all kindred hearts;
Ev'n thoſe, who fear his valour, love his vir-
tues.
Though thee we fear as our moſt deadly
foe,
Believe me, all thou now behold'ſt are friends.
Then ſtrive not, Cathmor, to conceal thy
griefs,

L l

From

From fympathizing hearts that wifh to fhare
them.

CATHMOR.

I wifh I could conceal my prefent griefs
Not only from my friends,—but from myfelf.

NATHOS.

Forgive me, Prince, if I conjecture wrong,
But fure thou haft much caufe of grief, and
feel'ft
Th' ungrateful ufage of thy barb'rous brother.

CATHMOR.

I feel it like a poifon'd arrow here !
Barb'rous indeed !——O Cairbar !——

NATHOS.

Could he feek
So brave a Prince's death ? Yet this appear'd
Plainly his treach'rous aim, in leaving thee
So few to meet our whole compacted force.

CATHMOR,

CATHMOR.

He promis'd to attack your rear, as foon
As I fhould charge your front :—He bafely
    fled,
And left me, as he thought, to fure deftruc-
    tion.

NATHOS.

You ftood like one regardlefs of his fate.

CATHMOR.

To find the zeal, the not unfruitful zeal,
With which I've ever ferv'd him, fo repaid,
So fhock'd and fo aftounded me, I ftood
Incapable of acting, till you brought
Your numbers round, and made me prifoner.

COLLA.

Whither has Cairbar with his army gone ?

CATHMOR.

I am not trufted now with Cairbar's coun-
    fels.

        NATHOS.

NATHOS.

Envious of glory which he ne'er can
    reach,
An enemy to virtues, which, compar'd
With his foul vices, make him look fo mean,
His little, bafe, malignant, rancorous mind
Has even attempted to deftroy a brother.
Confult thy fafety, Prince! Defend thyfelf
Againft an enemy, who threatens thee.

CATHMOR.

That threat'ning enemy is ftill my bro-
    ther.

NATHOS.

Ever a ftranger to th' endearing ties
Of brotherly affection, openly now
He by his deeds difclaims them: Join with
    us,
And in thy fervice I will die, or fet
Falfe Cairbar's crown on Cathmor's worthier
    brow.

CATHMOR.

CATHMOR.

You know not Cathmor.   He defires no
   crown
That one muft wade to thro' a brother's
   blood.

NATHOS.

At thine that very brother fcruples not,
Tho' there's no crown to tempt, no injury
T' excite revenge; and though thy ufeful
    life
Is cherifh'd and admir'd by all but him!
Does he, a wretch, whom all mankind deteft,
And juftly for his crimes condemn to death,
Deferve to wear a crown?—What thou haft
    fuffer'd
Calls loud for vengeance: but much more
    than that,
Thy future danger, and the care of life,
Which all are bound to have, admonifh thee
To ftand on thy defence againft this bro-
    ther.

CATHMOR.

CATHMOR.

Above the fervile fears of death, above
The mean ambition of inglorious greatnefs,
In fpite of his demerits, true to thofe
Dear feelings that connect fraternal hearts,
I will defend him, while my vigour lafts ;
And, fcorning crowns, afpire to brighter
    wreaths.

COLLA.

The fong, that fhall to future times record
This wondrous virtue, will by little fouls
Be deem'd romantic fable.

NATHOS.

                        But the brave
Inwardly confcious of refembling greatnefs,
Affenting, will extol th' accomplifh'd hero.
Take, gallant Cathmor ! take this fword,
    which fhines
With honour, even in a difhoneft caufe :
                [*Giving him his fword.*
And with it take thy freedom. Might I hope
                        Thy

Thy friendſhip in return, I would eſteem it
The richeſt ranſom ever captive paid.

CATHMOR.

If, by my friendſhip, thou mean'ſt that
    eſteem
Thy bravery merits, with a grateful ſenſe
Of this benevolence, thou haſt it now.——
But if thou giv'ſt me liberty, in hopes
That I ſhall draw this ſword againſt my bro-
    ther,
Thou art deceiv'd.——So take thy preſent
    back.
For in the battle I muſt be thy foe,
Whilſt thou art Cairbar's.

NATHOS.

That is, while either lives!
Without reſtraint, without conditions, free,
Obey the dictates of thy manly mind.
I know I put this weapon in a hand
That's terrible in battle: But I'm ſure,
I'll find one generous and one candid foe.

DARTHULA.

See one, whofe hafty fteps feem to foretel
His tidings are important.

NATHOS.

One of thofe
I fent to Cromla's top to look for Cairbar.

Enter a Meffenger.

MESSENGER.

Hafte, Nathos, hafte, with fuccours to thy
    brother.
Near Cormac's caftle he's with Cairbar met,
And much fuperior is the tyrant's force.

NATHOS.

All follow me.——Thou, Ardan only ftay,
With thy detachment.
             [*Exit with officers, &c.*

COLLA.

Ha! near Cormac's caftle.
                Bloody,

Bloody, I fear, is Cairbar's purpofe there.

DARTHULA.

Alas! my brother! Heavens protect the
King!

COLLA.

They're both in danger! But the caftle's
ftrong:
'Twill keep them out a while.

DARTHULA.

More news! More news!

COLLA.

Another meffenger from Cromla's heights!
What have you feen?

Enter another Meffenger.

MESSENGER.

Brave Athos form'd his troop
In a ftrait pafs 'twixt Cairbar and Temora.

M m   They

They met.—They clos'd: But foon they fe-
    parate.
And now that fide, which from its numbers
    feems
The enemy, is, by a quick retreat,
Haftening towards the caftle of the King.

COLLA.

'Tis fome bafe ftratagem to get admittance,
And murder Cormac.

DARTHULA.

       O my brother too!

COLLA.

Cairbar fpares none!—My Fruthil! O my
    fon!
My only fon! My only hope in age!
I will prevent their deaths, or die with them.
                   [*Exit.*

DARTHULA.

Stay, O my father! Stay, infirm old man!
                   Leave

Leave war's rough labours to more vigorous
    limbs !

[Exit.

CATHMOR, (alone.)

Ah Cormac ! could I yet prevent thy fate!
And Cairbar's fhame ! His name will be in-
    roll'd
Amongft the hated monfters of the earth!
'Twas plain he fought my life ! Shall I now
    fly
Where no foul rumour of his crimes can
    wound me ?
No ! I will go to him, and counteract
All his detefted deeds of infamy.

END OF THE FIRST ACT.

    CHORUS

CHORUS I.

SCENE—*Fingal's hall in Selma.*

Fingal, Offian, Nobles, Ladies, Bards, attending.

A difmal found is heard of diftant fhrieking.

FIRST BARD.

WHAT fhrieks !

SECOND BARD.

What hideous groans !

FINGAL.

I know too well !

FIRST BARD.

Some dire prefage !

SECOND BARD.

Some grief is nigh !

FINGAL.

FINGAL.

Some fpirits thus are wont to tell
When thofe moft dear to Fingal die.

FIRST BARD.

Felt ye that blaft?
How fwift it pafs'd!

SECOND BARD.

Methought it fhook the hall!

THIRD BARD.

What meteors there !
What lightnings blaze!

FIRST BARD.

Oh!—thefe portend
A king, or kingdom's fall!

OSSIAN.

Every breath new horror brings !
Hark, hark, my harp! no human hand
Has touch'd the ftrings!

That

That found fo difmal, hollow, low,
Foretells approaching news of woe!

FINGAL.

Strike, Offian! ftrike thy harp, my fon!
Call out the deep-refounding, folemn tone:
Sing on, till fome compaffionating ghoft
Come to tell what friends we've loft!

OSSIAN.

Spirits of our fathers dead!
   Whether ye glide
Smoothly o'er the cryftal waves;
Whether in the whirlwind's blaft,
   Ye roll the whitening tide;
Or pour the night-fhriek on the lonely hill;
  Or murmur o'er your graves!
 Come in your cloudy cars,
   And tell in founds of woe,
For what departed chiefs
   Muft our deep forrows flow!

CHORUS.

For what departed chiefs, &c.

OSSIAN.

OSSIAN.

Tell me of Ofcar, tell,
 Who fails the ftormy main :
Oh ! have you feen my darling fon
 Amid his martial train ?

Say, does brave Ofcar live ;
 Or are his fhips difpers'd,
And he, with all his band,
 In wat'ry tombs immers'd ?

Or have they reach'd green Uilin's fhores,
 And yet have come too late
To fave the fons of Ufnoth brave,
 And Cormac, from their fate ?

CHORUS.

Spirits of our fathers dead !
 Let us blind mortals know
For what departed chiefs
 Muft our deep forrows flow !

BARD

BÁRD OF THE SECOND SIGHT.

Ínvoke no ghoſts to teḷḷ you this!
Blindneſs, mòrtals, here is bliſs!
I ſee, I ſee, with inward light,
I ſee, and curſe the dire anticipated fight
   Which brings too ſoon my pain.
   I ſee, I ſee, beyond the deep
   A ſcene that ſhall make thouſands weep!

CHORUS FIRST.

What ſcene?

CHORUS SECOND.

What ſcene?

CHORUS THIRD.

What ſcene?

BÁRD.

Ye hear the ſhrieks! I ſee the ghoſts!
Trembling they come from Erin's coaſts,
Deterr'd by bloody horrors thence!

CHORUS

CHORUS FIRST.

What blood? What horror? Tell the worſt!

CHORUS SECOND.

Speak, ſpeak!

CHORUS THIRD.

Oh ſpeak, we're all ſuſpence!

BARD.

Oſcar is ſafe! He holds his way!
Tight are his ſhips, his warriors gay!
They ſoon ſhall land ;—and yet too late;
The ſons of Uſnoth too are well!
The reſt, the reſt, oh urge me not to tell!

CHORUS.

Oh! tell the worſt of Fate!

BARD.

Oh horror! murder! ſight of woe!

N n   CHORUS.

CHORUS.

Tell, oh tell us, all you know.

BARD.

Look not now on Ullin's fhore!
   See ye not the ftreaming gore?
   Erin's young nobles now no more
   Shall Erin's expectations raife!
   Cormac and his youthful peers
   Sporting with their fathers fpears
   Practife the feats of riper years!
Their little bofoms feel the warrior's flame!
Their little bofoms feaft on future fame!
   But death's dark night the whole deftroys!

CHORUS.

Death's dark night the whole deftroys?

BARD.

Cairbar! Atha's gloomy Lord,
Wherefore doft thou draw the fword?
Murderer! Coward! They are boys!

CHORUS.

CHORUS.

Is there no hand to fave? no fword
To ftrike the murderers and prevent the blow?

BARD.

There is no hand to fave, or fword!
  Ghofts that glut in human gore,
  Grimly glooming, ftalk before!
  Murder grins at every door!
    Fly! They cannot fly!
In heaps they fall!—they die?—they fall,
  Murder'd in Temora's hall!
  Erin's youthful nobles, all
    Around poor Cormac lie!

CHORUS.

Murder'd in Temora's hall
  With murder'd Cormac die?

BARD.

Cormac lives yet! The fword is rais'd!
  What gallant youth art thou,

That

That interceptſt the falling edge?—
  Oh moſt unworthy blow!

Though generouſly, though nobly done,
  Thou giv'ſt thy king but ſhort relief!
  O heart-confounding grief!
'Tis Colla's ſon!

CHORUS.

His only ſon?

BARD.

With his lov'd Prince he leaves the light!
He dies! his morning ſun is ſet in endleſs
    night.

CHORUS.

Cormac and Colla's only ſon!
Alas! their days were ſcarce begun!

BARD.

The murd'rous ſcene is done?

CHORUS.

CHORUS.

What wonder that afflicted ghosts
Fly from these unhappy coasts?
What wonder that all nature mourn'd?
   That harps spontaneous moan;
That distant hills felt and return'd
   Their dying groan!
A deed so horrible, so foul, was never told
By modern Seer, or Bard of old!

FINGAL.

In sweetly-soothing, melancholy strains
   Sing, Ossian, to their gentle spirits sing!
Allay the anguish of their dying pains!
   Let them with joy to their new mansions
      spring!

OSSIAN.

Descend to greet them, friendly shades
   Of kindred gone before!
Conduct them, wond'ring and afraid,
   The regions new t' explore!

Rise,

Rife, gentle, ftranger fpirits, rife!
  Pain ye no more fhall know ;
In leaving life's uncertain joys,
  Ye leave its certain woe !

Ye cannot fee, indeed, your names
  Among the great inroll'd ;
But thorny are the paths to fame ;
  And few are blefs'd when old !

Your fathers bleeding hearts, alas !
  Which fondly once conceiv'd
The hopes that you fhould fill their place,
  Are of all hopes bereav'd !

But had they died, like you, when young,
  They now had foundly flept,
They had not flourifh'd in the fong,
  Nor for their children wept !

CHORUS

Spirits of Erin ! ceafe to mourn !
  Too late ye our affiftance feek!
Home to your airy dwellings turn ;
  No more on Morven's mountains fhriek !

FINGAL.

FINGAL.

Call in the wreftlers from the green,
　　The nimble hunters from the heath!
Shall we in idle fports be feen ?
　　No—Let us hafte t'avenge their death !

CHORUS.

Spirits of Erin fpeed the happy gales !
　　Strengthen each fav'ring current and cach
　　　　wave !
Fly fwiftly homeward on our fwelling fails !
　　Hafte to avenge the dead, and the furvi-
　　　　vors fave !

ACT

A C T II.

SCENE.—*A court within the gates of Cormac's castle.*

CAIRBAR.

YOU whining bards, in your pedantic
    rhimes,
Will blazon this action with opprobrious
    titles.
Rail on, rail on !—By this am I become
The sole great Sovereign of this spacious isle!
When one attains what he with ardour wish'd,
Should not his joy of satisfaction rise
In lively transports ? I feel no such thing !
But rather something ever stinging me ;
For I have done what all will execrate.

Enter

Enter Althan.

ALTHAN.

Turn, murderer! hither turn, and end thy
  works!

CAIRBAR.

Where are my guards? Why am I left alone?

ALTHAN.

The guilty tremble when no danger's near;
And well mayft thou, whom deeds inhuman
  mark
The common enemy of human kind.

CAIRBAR.

Thou art not worth my notice!—Live, old
  bard,
And fing this fcene that makes me king of
  Erin.

ALTHAN.

And art thou fo depraved to boaft of it?

O o   It

It fhall be fung—But O what words çan
    paint
Its difmal horrors? All our once great hopes
Of rifing heroes murder'd with their king.
Their fhrieks and groans fhook Erin's hardeft
    rocks;
Pierc'd the deep caverns of the folid earth,
Th' abyffes of th' unfathom'd ocean, rous'd
The fpirits of the long-departed dead;
Moving all things but thy unnatural heart.

CAIRBAR.

Think'ft thou I would be mov'd by chil-
    dren's fcreams,
When th' empire of all Erin was in view.
Go, fing Temora's crown to Alnecma's join'd,
By mighty Cairbar, the firft King of Erin.

ALTHAN.

Thou King of Erin!——Rather may the
    waves,
That round her confines beat, meet in the
    center,
And leave no hill to tell where Erin ftood.

CAIRBAR.

CAIRBAR.

Wilt thou compel me yet to murder thee?

ALTHAN.

Yes, ftrike!——What is an old man's ufe-
    lefs life,
After the youthful lives by thee deftroy'd?——
Tyrant of Erin fhort while fhalt thou be!
Vengeance is near thee!——I have heard thy
    doom!
Their fathers ghofts, who at their murder
    groan'd,
Bear it with awful gladnefs through the fky,
And frown revengeful o'er thy deftin'd head.

CAIRBAR.

My death canft thou forefee, and not thine
    own,
Which is much nearer thee?

GATHMOR, (*entering*.)

          Hold, Cairbar, hold!
O o 2   Hold!

Hold! Too much murder thou to-day haſt
    done:
Though not ſo much as thou didſt meditate.

CAIRBAR.

Welcome, my brother, from the dangerous
    field?

CATHMOR.

Dangerous indeed!—as thou hadſt plann'd
    the fight.

CAIRBAR.

I thought—Believe me—I have been de-
    ceiv'd——
I was inform'd——A ſtronger army 'twas—

CATHMOR.

No more of that!——I would forget.thy
    baſeneſs:
But in too faſt ſucceſſion come thy crimes,
And ſtill the laſt is the moſt infamous.
What could provoke thee now to raiſe the
    ſword

                        Over

Over this hoary head? this facred head,
In which are regifter'd the glorious feats
Of antient chiefs, with thofe who lately fell?
And grateful fongs are forming now to fire
Our laft defcendants with our prefent fame!

ALTHAN.

But it were well for him that Fame were
mute;
That all records fhould with his being ceafe,
And with his carcafe all remembrance rot.

CAIRBAR.

You fee, my brother, how I am contemn'd!
And am I brought fo low to fuffer this?

CATHMOR.

Contempt will ever be the lot of vice,
However high in ftation! If thou fear'ft
The free reproach of independent Bards,
Deferve it not.—Thou murder'ft Cathmor's
fame!
When laid in earth, they'll fay, " He fought
" for Cairbar!"

No

No song shall rise, no tear fall o'er his tomb.

CAIRBAR.

How beautiful, my brother, are thy vir-
    tues!
How foul my vices, when compar'd with
    them?
But now, possess'd of all ambition wish'd,
(Since Erin all from sea to sea is mine,)
I will from henceforth strive to imitate
Thy worth, and rise by virtuous deeds to fame.

CATHMOR.

I've little faith in this!—Nathos advances
With all his army! Shall we wait him here?
Or sallying out attack him on the plain?

CAIRBAR.

Here we will stay to night: The castle's
    strong.
See if the gates be shut, and guards prepared.
       [*Exeunt Cathmor, Althan.*

CAIRBAR *(alone.)*

In spite of me, his virtues I approve,

                  And

And whilſt with him in my reſolves t'amend
I almoſt am ſincere. But when he's gone
My own more profitable views return.
When will thy fooliſh virtues bring a crown?
And yet they might! He is belov'd by all!
And I am hated!—He has ſeen my aim!
How has it fail'd! It was, it ſeems, too groſs
Even to deceive his unſuſpecting foul!—
He's dangerous? No peace I'll ever find,
Till I am ſooth'd with Cathmor's funeral
  ſong!

Enter Cathmor.

CATHMOR.

Old Colla with his daughter is without:
He begs permiſſion to convey the bodies
Of his own ſon, his king, and other nobles,
With decent obſequies to humble tombs.

CAIRBAR.

Darthula too? Yes, Cathmor, bring them
  in:
Aſſure them of my real penitence;

        Of

Of lenient entertainment while they're here,
And liberty at pleafure to depart.

CATHMOR.

And may I truft you are fincere in this?

CAIRBAR.

Sincere, my brother, as I mean t' amend.

[*Exit Cathmor.*

CAIRBAR *(alone.)*

Good fortune pours on me! Darthula here,
Where I am fovereign? No! I'll ufe no force!
She muft defire to be fo great a queen;
And that may pleafe th' ambitious father too!
They muft not fee me in this bloody trim!
In fmootheft language I'll entreat them both.

[*Exit.*

Enter Colla, Darthula, Althan.

COLLA.

Why did ye not, ye facred towers of Cormac,

Fall

Fall on the murderer's heads? Were ye awake
Avenging fpirits? You who tempefts raife,
And dart red thunder! ah! had ye no pow'r
To tear his limbs, and hurl his curfed foul
Into the darkeft dungeon of defpair?

ALTHAN.

Why enters Colla thefe unhappy gates!

COLLA.

Althan! How did the villain pity thee?
Did he not pity Fruthil too and Cormac?
Did he relent? and are they yet in life?

ALTHAN.

Why came you hither? Your own life's in
danger.

COLLA.

My life!—O 'tis too long!—For what great
crimes
Am I referv'd the laft of all my race?
Was it in light? Had they the fhapes of men

P p

That

That kill'd fuch innocents?——Didft thou
    behold it?
And did thine eyes not from their fockets
    leap?
Ah! how could'ft thou fupport a fight fo
    fhocking?

ALTHAN.

Two of his ruffians held me in the cham-
    ber,
A forc'd fpectator of the bafeft murder
That e'er difgrac'd the chronicles of men.

COLLA.

Defcribe it black in all its fhocking hor-
    rors!
And let my foul's high indignation fwell,
Till thefe old heart-ftrings with the paffion
    break!

ALTHAN.

This villain, who did never any act
But by fome fordid ftratagem, in hafte,
As if purfu'd, with all his army fought

A

A refuge for the vanquifh'd troops of Nathos.
We let him in, tho' loud the ravens croak'd,
And howling dogs beheld the trembling
    ghofts,
That came with fhrieks to warn us of the
    woe.
But fee he comes.

DARTHULA.

Where fhall I fly from him?—
Conduct me, Althan, where the haplefs boys
Yet ghaftly in their wounds all bloody lie.

ALTHAN.

Ah, Lady, 'tis a fight of frightful horror!

DARTHULA.

'Tis not fo frightful as the fight of Cairbar.
      [*Exeunt Darthula and Althan.*

           Colla

Colla and Cairbar.

COLLA.

Come Cairbar! Murderer come! Here is a
    breaſt
Will thank the friendly arm that pierces it!

CAIRBAR.

Nothing has Colla t' apprehend from me!
Nothing but good mean I to thee and thine!
I've long eſteem'd thy merit, long deſir'd
To be inroll'd among the happy number
Of Colla's friends.

COLLA.

       What? Comes the carion-crow,
In blood of the devoured lamb beſinear'd,
With ſhow of friendſhip, to decoy the dame?

CAIRBAR.

Here I am King, and can command thy
  death!

COLLA.

COLLA.

That here thou'rt King is worfe to me than
  death !

CAIRBAR.

I wifh'd to be a King for Colla's fake !
That he might fhare with me the fovereign
  pow'r.
I wifh'd for empire, that I might appear
More worthy of the love of fair Darthula.

COLLA.

Moft likely means to win a virgin's love !——
Go, warm in Fruthil's blood, and woe his
  fifter !
Vaunt of thy valour, that could, unprovok'd,
Butcher defencelefs infants ! Shew the fpoils
Stol'n from Temora's ftores, and tell her,
  thefe
Have made thee worthy of Darthula's love !

CAIRBAR.

Was thy fon there?——Oh my unlucky arm !
                                    Forgive

Forgive me, Colla! No! I knew him not,
In that occasion which ambition found
To attain that empire I so ardent wish'd.

COLLA.

Ambition! Wretch! It was thy avarice,
The lucre, not the glory of a crown,
Tempted thy little soul to such a crime!
Ambition never kept so foul a seat
As thy base heart.

CAIRBAR.

No matter what it was.——
You and your daughter both are in my pow'r.
Do you consent that she shall be my Queen?

COLLA.

No!——Colla's blood shall never mix with
Cairbar's.

CAIRBAR.

What! Would not Cairbar's blood ennoble
Colla's!
My fathers long have fill'd Alnecma's throne,
And

And made your monarchs of the north to
    tremble.

COLLA.

I knew thy father well!—Fierce Borbur-
    duthil,
Like thee, delighted in the bloody field,
When feeble foes with little danger fell.
But he had pride, and never would have
    stoop'd
To such degrading deeds of infamy.
If Cairbar's brood degenerate as much,
They'll soon depopulate the living world.

CAIRBAR.

Guards!——Take this ill-tongu'd traitor
    from my sight;
And let him in some vault unheeded rail.

COLLA, (*drawing his sword.*)

I've seen the day!——But twenty years
    ago,
All these had fled like herds of timorous deer.
                  Revenge,

Revenge, give vigour!

[*Attacking Cairbar, and is unarmed.*

     Curfe my feeble limbs!

Had thefe obey'd the impulfe of my foul,

His hated blood had now fmoak'd on the
  pavement;

And peftilence, fprung from the filthy fteams,

Had wafted half the world. Slaves! take me
  hence!

     · [*Exit guarded.*

CAIRBAR, (*alone.*)

Enlarg'd dominion, wealth, and pow'r in-
  creas'd,

I find have only brought me more contempt.

'Tis true, I am a villain, and deferve not

Real refpect: But fuch have found it fha-
  dowed

In th' adulation of mens hopes and fears.——

I know this makes me not more amiable

In female eyes. But there are many,

Who, for diffembled homage, forc'd refpect,

And all th' external pageantry of ftate,

Would fhare with me thefe inward pangs of
  confcience.

       Darthula

Darthula may be one of thofe! I'll try it!—
Oh! fhe deferves the greateft monarch's love!

Enter Darthula.

DARTHULA.

My father bound! Thou murderer of my
    brother!
Thou wilt not kill my aged father too!

CAIRBAR.

No violence to Colla or to thee
Do I intend.——The old man was incens'd.
I but fecur'd him by a fhort confinement,
Until his dangerous frenzy fhall fubfide.
But how fhall I with love accoft Darthula,
Whom I have injur'd thus? Oh, blinded eyes!
Could ye not in her brother's features fee
Some fweet refemblance of Darthula's charms!
Charms, that through night's obfcurity might
    fend
Meridian luftre!—Ah could Cairbar's tears
Recal him back to life! Thefe tears fhould
    flow

Q q

Till

Till Cairbar wafted in the bitter flood !

DARTHULA.

This grief fictitious, thefe diffembled tears,
Thefe fighs conftrain'd, and this pretended
    fawning,
Can ne'er impofe on me; for through them
    all
I fee thy little foul ftill brooding o'er
Its wonted murders, rapine, and deceit.

CAIRBAR.

Miftaken, cruel fair one ! Could'ft thou fee
My foul aright, thou'd'ft fee it all contrition;
All chang'd to pity, foften'd and prepar'd
To be new modell'd by Darthula's will !
For day and night I've conftant figh'd for thee,
Since firft I faw thee ! O the fweet remem-
    brance !
'Twas when Alnecma once with Ullin met
In peaceful fports, to try their heroes ftrength.
The plain was circled by a ring of beauty,
Like that which oft arrays the fhowery fphere:
Thou, like the fun gav'ft luftre to the whole;
In youthful charms bright as the morning fun,
                When

When firſt he ſmiles upon the ſettled lake!
When firſt the riſing fiſhes leap for joy,
And birds on bordering buſhes ſweetly ſing.
On thee engaging champions caſt their eyes,
And felt new vigour from th' inſpiring view;
Their looks on thee the bards tranſported fix'd;
And when they ſhould have ſung the conque-
  ror's praiſe,
Their erring tongues pronounc'd Selama's
  maid.
Love's flames ſince that time in my boſom
  burn'd.
O! be the Queen of Erin and of Cairbar!

DARTHULA.

Sooner I'd leap into the angry mouths
Of bears or wolves. I'd ſooner meet grim
  death
In the moſt dreadful form e'er terror fancy'd.

CAIRBAR.

I like no bear or wolf purſue to tear thee!
I woe thee gently to thy happineſs.

    DAR-

DARTHULA.

Like bear or wolf!—Like Cairbar!—That
　　is worfe.
They fpare the young of their peculiar kinds;
But he's a monfter of fome new fierce kind,
Which nature knows not yet, and has not
　　nam'd.

CAIRBAR.

Blufhing, I own I have too long been fuch.
Chang'd by my love, I'm now all gentlenefs:
My melting heart expands itfelf to thee,
And would inclofe thee in its inmoft folds.
As the fun's warmth firft forms the fwelling
　　buds,
Then makes the fragrant bloffoms of the
　　fpring,
With heat accumulated, grow to fruit;
So fhall my love——

DARTHULA.

　　　　Peace, vile diffembler! Peace!
The fierceft tempeft of the frozen North
Ne'er made fuch havoc on the blooming fpring,
　　　　　　　　　　　　　　　As

As thou haſt done on Erin's richeſt bloſſoms.
Hear me, departed ſpirits of my brothers!
If I conſent to love your murderer,
That inſtant ſend me ſome more torturing
    death,
Than mortals know; and when my body's
    cold,
Deſpiſe my ſpirit; ſpurn it far from you,
To howl with the oppreſſors of mankind,
Who on each other in grim Torture's cave
Practiſe the dreadful parts they play'd in life!

CAIRBAR.

Yet, yet relent! Think what is in my
    pow'r!
To make thee Queen of this extenſive iſle,
Or make thee priſoner, and take by force—
Why this intruſion?

Enter Cathmor.

CATHMOR.

Wherefore am I made
The ſhameful inſtrument of your deceit?
                                    You

You made me now affure them, ere they en-
    tered,
Of gentle treatment while they tarried here,
And liberty at pleafure to depart.
Yet Colla you have made a prifoner;
And in the lady's face I read diftrefs!

CAIRBAR.

I am thy King.

CATHMOR.

    Thou art my brother too.
But make me not forget that double bond.

CAIRBAR.

His boldnefs awes me. (*afide.*)——No my
    beft of friends,
No more fhall Cairbar's conduct give thee pain.
Go, fet old Colla free.——This fcornful fair,
Safe in the ftrength of her all-pow'rful charms,
Needs nothing fear. In fofteft terms of love,
I woo'd her to be Erin's Queen and mine.

CATHMOR.

Nathos has fent a party, who demand
                The

The bodies of th' unhappy youths, to lay
Among their fathers, with th' accuftom'd
    rites.
That done, he'll meet thee on th' adjacent
    plain.
To avenge, he fays, their deaths, or fhare
    their fates.

CAIRBAR.

The bodies let him have. Their fates he'll
    fhare.
And fo I'll tell him. Cathmor, follow me.
        [*Exeunt Cairbar and Cathmor.*

DARTHULA, (*alone.*)

Tremendous Pow'rs! who fierce in hurri-
    canes,
Or fwifter thunders, dart th' avenging ftroke!
Why is the foreft, or th' unfeeling rock
Rent in your idle wrath, while Cairbar lives?

Enter

Enter Colla.

COLLA.

Break! break? Wilt thou not break, my
stubborn heart?

DARTHULA.

What means my father?

COLLA.

Wherefore have I liv'd?
Wherefore, O wherefore, have I liv'd to see
The laſt of all my ſons borne to his grave?

DARTHULA.

Ah!——Are they gone?

COLLA.

Now they are carrying out.
My King! My ſon! How ghaſtly in their
wounds!
And of brave youths untimely ſlain, beſides,

More

More than enough to break the hardeſt heart,
Although no ſon of mine, or King, were
    there:
Yet mine breaks not.

DARTHULA.

Let us go hence, my father.

COLLA.

Yes; we will follow the ſad ſpectacle,
And leave this diſmal, now deteſted place.
Once happy ſeat of royal dignity,
Art thou become the nauſeous den of mur-
    der?
        [*Going, they are ſtopt by a guard.*

GUARD.

I am commanded to detain you here.

DARTHULA.

'Tis as I fear'd!——He will not let us go,

COLLA.

He by our danger will reſtrain the rage
      R r   Of

Of fuch as would revenge the death of Cormac.

DARTHULA.

Our danger!——O, my father! great our
danger.

Enter Cairbar.

COLLA.

Tyrant! What is thy bloody purpofe now?

CAIRBAR.

Much I repent me of the blood I've fhed,
But hope to be compell'd to fhed no more.
If Colla, yet rejoicing long in life,
Would fee his daughter Erin's happy Queen—
If thou would'ft fmile in thy departing hour,
To think that Princes fhall defcend of thee;
Solicit her t' accept my offer'd love.

COLLA.

Behold a father on his bended knee,
To entreat his daughter.

DAR-

DARTHULA.

What can my father mean?

COLLA.

By thy departed mother's shade, whose
    charms
Now seem renew'd in thee! By those dear
    shades,
That yet are hovering o'er their bleeding
    limbs,
New borne to burial! I conjure thee——

DARTHULA.

              What?

COLLA.

Despise the murderer!—Scorn all shame-
    ful greatness!

DARTHULA.

Thou know'st me not, if thou hast any
    fears.

          COLLA.

COLLA.

I fear not that his greatnefs, or his love,
Difplay'd with all his art, fhall ever find
A traitor weaknefs in my daughter's heart.
But fhould he with his wonted rigour threat
This hoary head; refufe, and let me die!

CAIRBAR.

Then die thou muft. Ha! Can I be refus'd
Where all is in my pow'r?

DARTHULA.

     My life's in mine!——
My father rife!—Why didft thou kneel to
 pray
To her thou may'ft command?

COLLA.

     I've more to beg!
Should he compel thee to his hated bed,
Let never fleep or flumber fhut thine eye,
Till, in fome heedlefs hour, thou make his blood
       Attone

Attone for murder'd Fruthil's, and thy King's.

CAIRBAR, *(putting his hand to his sword.)*

Ha!—Suffer this! Old traitor, doſt thou
    hatch
Thy dangerous treaſons in a Sovereign's hear-
    ing?
No!—I'll be merciful!——Go: Take him
    hence!
And in ſome ſtrong apartment ſhut him up.

COLLA.

Tear me, thou tyrant! tear me limb from
    limb:
But from my dear, dear daughter drag me
    not.
               [*He is forced out.*

DARTHULA.

Let me be laid with him in ſome dark
    vault;
And let us die together far from thee.

CAIRBAR.

No!—This apartment, Lady, is thine own.
Or, when thou pleafeft, walk through all this
   court.
Hear this you guards!——Still keep within
   her fight.

Enter Althan.

ALTHAN.

Wilt thou confine the Lady?

CAIRBAR.

                    Worthy bard,
Stay thou with her.   If by thy foftening arts
Of mufic, thou canft foothe her cruel heart,
Thou fhalt be firft of all the bards of Erin.

ALTHAN.

Not from the favour of a tyrant comes
The bard's pre-eminence. The tuneful pow'rs
Diftinguifh them. Men yet unborn may glow
                                    — With

With Althan's fong! But none fhall ever fay,
He flatter'd vice, tho' crown'd with bound-
. lefs pow'r. •

CAIRBAR.

Then ftarve on airy fame,—thou whining
fool!
In manlier founds thus Cairbar fings his love:
I give thee yet an hour to think of it.——
If then thou ftill refufe to be my Queen,
Thy father, that old ftubborn fool fhall die.
I'll cut his gray head from his ftooping fhoul-
ders.
And when thou haft beheld the dreadful
fcene,
Force fhall procure what is deny'd to love.

[*Exit.*

Darthula, Althan, Guards.

DARTHULA.

Thou monfter! Force?—O had he threatned death,

I

I could have fmil'd at the uplifted fword;
Receiv'd its fall without a dying groan,
And gone a joyful ghoft to meet my bro-
    thers.
Within an hour! Thefe guards, thefe guards
    oppofe.

ALTHAN.

Aye, they prevent it: Elfe I could thee
    lead
Without his pow'r.

DARTHULA.

        O tell me, Althan, how.
To leap from th' higheft of this caftle's walls,
Into its deepeft ditch, and fink in mud,
Compos'd of filth and putrid carcafes,
Were far lefs horrible than ftaying here.

ALTHAN.

Some lucky moment we perhaps may find,
When they fhall in their vigilance relax.—

DARTHULA.

And is it but perhaps?—Our time runs on!
                  Stern

Stern perpetrators of his cruelties,
Whose swords are reeking yet with childrens
blood!
To murder me would show some pity in you.
If any more humane.—But Cathmore comes.
Cathmor is merciful! He'll give me death!

Enter Cathmor.

Does Cathmor bear his brothers harsh com-
    mands,
To aggravate my sorrows?

CATHMOR.

                      No, Darthula!
I sympathize with thee in all thy sorrows,
And hate, like thee, my brother's shameful
    deeds.
Before you entered these unhappy gates,
He made me pledge my honour for your
    safety.
Though he meant to deceive, I was sincere;
And still look on myself as bound to exert
My power to frustrate his base stratagems.

DAR-

Vile and contemptible mankind would be,
Were all like Cairbar! But the few like Cath-
    mor
Still make us of our general nature proud.
Moſt generous friend of men! thy chiefeſt
    joy
Is ſtill in actions of benevolence,
Relieving the diſtreſs'd of every kind!
Greater diſtreſs ne'er ſtood before thee, Cath-
    mor!
Than now thou feeſt. One hour, and that
    runs on,
'Twixt threatned force and murder!—Save,
    O ſave me!

CATHMOR.

Point out ſome way. By force I cannot
    now:
And with his nature ſupplication's vain.

DARTHULA.

No ſupplication can have weight with him!
                      He

He knows no love, no pity, no remorfe,
None of th' affections that the virtuous feel.
For hatred, envy, malice, and revenge,
With falfehood, avarice, and cruelty,
Are all th' ingredients of his dark'ned foul.

CATHMOR.

Canft thou, O reverend bard, devife no
means?

ALTHAN.

I know a paffage, and 'tis known to few,
By which, but for thefe guards, we might
efcape.

DARTHULA.

Their orders are, ne'er to lofe fight of us.
And could I leave my poor old father here?

ALTHAN.

If there's a meffenger that you could truft,
This way he might bring Nathos in with
force,

S s 2
That

That by furprize could drive out Cairbar's
    troops.

CATHMOR.

I've no fuch meffenger! No friend of mine
Whom I could truft, has entred yet thefe
    walls.
Important is the truft!

DARTHULA.

            Our time is fhort!

CATHMOR.

But this attempt were to betray my bro-
    ther,
Elfe would I be this meffenger myfelf.

DARTHULA.

Does fuch a brother merit Cathmor's love?
Then love thy brother, and prevent his
    fhame!
And O remember, that our little hour
Is almoft half expir'd!

CATHMOR.

CATHMOR.

There is no way
To fave you, but by bringing Nathos in :
And his refentment would not fpare my bro-
ther.

DARTHULA.

Yes! he will fpare him for brave Cathmor's fake.
Make thefe conditions with him firft.

CATHMOR.

I will.
Where is this paffage? Under ground, I hope.

ALTHAN.

In yonder vault, whofe entrance fronts us
here,
You near the middle of the floor will find
A ring. That pulls a trap door up. Go down.
The way is fmooth and eafy. Four in rank,
Marching upright, may carry all their
arms.

DAR-

DARTHULA.

O generous Cathmor, fly with swiftest
    speed,
Lest Cairbar come, and blast our new-sprung
    hopes :
As frost the forward bud which comes too
    early,
With the deceitful warmth of winter suns.

CATHMOR.

If Cairbar come, seem to consent to love
    him;
Or make excuses for some short delay.

                        [*Exit.*

DARTHULA.

Seem to consent !——I'm yet untaught to
    seem.
My looks with falsehood never will accord.
My tongue, as yet unpractis'd in deceit,
Will, fault'ring, all the blameless fraud be-
    tray.
By fair resistance may I not evade him,
                         Till

Till Nathos come?

Then will he kill thy father.

DARTHULA.

O had I never been, or dy'd a child,
My father thou hadſt liv'd in ſafety now!
In half an hour! Muſt I be forc'd to ſee
My venerable father dragg'd to death?
He threat'ned worſe!——Diſtraction! Never,
      never!
With my own hand I'll liberate my ſoul!

ALTHAN.

Hope ſtill the beſt! Cathmor is ſwift of
      foot.
He'll run with ſpeed, and Nathos will re-
      turn
Upon love's ſwifteſt wings to ſave Darthula.

DAR-

DARTHULA.

Soon he may come too late !

ALTHAN.

O'ercome your fears,
And go within; left in your anxious looks
Thefe prying guards find matter of fufpi-
cion.

[*Exeunt.*

END OF THE SECOND ACT.

C H O R U S II.

SCENE, *A burying place near Nathos' army.*

NATHOS, OFFICERS, BARDS, MUSICIANS.

I.

FAREWELL! Alas! a long farewell;
   Too tender tenants of a tomb!
By murder's stern commands ye fell;
   Fell ere your lives had reach'd their bloom.
How savage he who so commands!
     And cruel, cruel they,
Whose harden'd hearts allow their hands,
     Such stern commands to obey!
   Now, lifeless, breathless, cold,
   Laid low beneath the mold,
    In the damp ground,
    Ye sleep profound:

T t

While

While bufy life is buftling round,
And fears and fell remorfe the murderers
    wound,
  Here your fair limbs muft now decay,
And all remembrance of you fade away.

II.

Yet many long, with heart-fprung tears,
  Unhappy Cormac's fate fhall mourn,
And long lament the little Peers
  That were about, his reign t' adorn.
Your mournful fathers long for you
  Shall heave the fecret figh;
And long your mother's tears bedew
  The pillows where they lie.
      Oft hither fhall repair
      The little virgins fair,
        Their griefs to fhew,
        And round you ftrew
The fweeteft flowers their fancies know,
While down their lovely cheeks the bitter tor-
    rents flow;
  And every little bofom heaves,
To fee their brothers, or young lovers graves.

III. But

III.

But raife, bleft fouls, your fpiritual eyes!
Behold the wonders of the fkies!
The fpirits of your grandfires old,
Although we cannot, ye behold!
Thofe fpirits kind, that wont erewhile,
On all your little plays to fmile;
That lately at your murder frown'd,
That groan'd and wept at ev'ry wound:
Affembled by your fing'lar fate,
Now all in fmiles around you wait.
They wait, till they have heard our fong,
To lead your tim'rous fouls along.
To teach you on new wings to fly
Through the new pleafures of the fky.
 Faint is their voice! It founds too low
  For a grofs mortal ear;
 But fp'ritual language now ye know;
  Now ye thefe friendly greetings hear:

IV.

 " Welcome ev'ry gentle fhade,
 " Welcome here to better life!

T t 2   " Ye

" Ye leave the world; but are ye therefore
  " fad?

" Ye leave much anguifh, terror, envy, ftrife!
  " Fear no more the murderer's blow!

  " Sorrows ye no more fhall know.

  " On generous fouls we ever fmile,

  " And lead them to fublimeft joys;

" But fordid minds, whom cruel deeds defile,

" We all contend to humble and defpife.

  " If ye bring with you inward peace;

  " Everlafting is your blifs!

" In youth's moft pleafant playful days,

  " With health and vigour ye arrive;

" To health more certain, to more pleafant
  " plays,

" And never-ending youth ye now revive!

  " Rife, happy fpirits! chearful rife,

  " To moft fublime etherial joys!

V.

  " Does Cormac all his courtiers bring,

  " His life's companions in his train?

  " Moft happy courtiers! happy King!

  " Begin, begin your happy reign!

         " No

" No wrangling jealous fear,
" No envying even of fav'rites here!
" But ev'ry mind ferene, and ev'ry confcience
    " clear!

VI.

" Behold the joys fublime of light!
" Behold thefe cloud-form'd fteeds, with
    " wings of wind;
" With all the rainbow's colours bright!
" Swift as the quick emotions of the mind!
" Our thoughts at once rife to the moon!
" Thofe little airy fteeds can thither fly as
    " foon!
" D'ye choofe the chace? or mimic war?
" On thefe you'll bound from ftar to ftar!
" Would ye fee whence fprings the foremoft ray
    " Of morning light?
" Or the dark cave where refts by day,
    " The gloomy night?
" On thefe o'er earth, o'er feas, o'er ether
    " foar,
" All nature's wondrous myfteries at once ex-
    " plore!

VII. " But

VII.

" But if it more fhall pleafe
   " To vifit earth below ;
" Your mournful parents hearts to eafe
   " Of wafting woe :
" Gently, gently on their flumbers fteal ;
" Difturb them not with fudden fcreams :
" But in foftly-foothing dreams,
   " Their bleeding forrows heal.

VIII.

" If ye fometimes wifh in your wrath
   " Due vengeance for your wrongs to find,
" Wifh not for the curs'd murderer's death ;
   " But view his tortur'd mind !
" See,—for ye now can fee it plain,
" What phantoms rack the guilty brain !
" Short fleeps !—dire dreams !—He ftarts, he
    " wakes !
" He at imagin'd horror fhakes !
" Remorfe and never-ceafing fear
" Engender ftill frefh pois'nous fnakes,
   " His confcious breaft to tear !

                        " By

" By tortur'd mortals pangs fevere are felt!
" But there's no torture like the fting of guilt."

Enter Cathmor haftily.

CATHMOR.

Th' importance of my meffage will excufe
   me,
For interrupting thus your pious rites!
O Nathos, hear!—Meantime caufe light fome
   torches.

(*Cathmor and Nathos walk afide, while the
   Chorus goes off finging.*)

CHORUS.

Forever! ever!—O farewell!
  Forever, deareft youths, adieu!
Yet future bards your fates may tell,
  And future mourners weep for you!
    Forever, O adieu!
        [*Exeunt Chorus.*

Manent

Manent Cathmor, Nathos, Officers.

CATHMOR.

I know he will not fight thee. 'Tis agreed
That he fhall go in fafety with his troops.

NATHOS.

Not one fhall fall, if they make no refift-
    ance.——
O my Darthula! what thou fuffer'ft now!——
My Caledonians only follow me.——
Four men in rank. One torch muft go before.
Difpofe the reft fo as t' enlight the whole!
    [*Exit with Cathmor foldiers bearing torches.*

Remain fome Erinian officers.

FIRST OFFICER.

His Caledonians! So! 'Tis manifeft
We are not trufted by our foreign chief!

SECOND OFFICER.

A fmooth-fac'd boy to lead fuch veteran
    warriors.   [*Exeunt.*
                ACT

ACT III.

Scene within the Caftle, as before.

Cairbar meeting an Officer.

OFFICER.

CATHMOR we cannot find.

CAIRBAR.

    Search all the apartments.
Laft night he watch'd ; was much fatigu'd to-
  day,
And now perhaps he is retir'd to reft.——
Were I affur'd that he would ne'er be found,
'Twould give me little forrow. But I fear
We foon fhall find him with our enemy,
And thither all our force will follow him,——
I am no king while this fmooth Cathmor lives!
Who faw my brother laft ?

     U u   OFFICER

OFFICER ON GUARD.

I faw him lately
Converfing with the mourning lady here.
'Twas when you left her. Both appear'd dif-
   turb'd,
She with her fears, and he with fympathy.
Their conference was fhort; but it feem'd
   earneft.
I ftood too far remote to hear their words.

CAIRBAR.

What! is Darthula gone along with him?

OFFICER.

As you commanded, we kept fight of her;
Nor has fhe yet from this apartment ftirr'd.

CAIRBAR.

And if fhe be not there, woe to thy life!
I'll ihftantly be fatisfy'd of this.
                    [*Opening the door.*

DAR-

DARTHULA, (*rushing out in fear.*)

What would'st thou now? The time is not
expir'd.

CAIRBAR, (*after a pause.*)

Be all the guards,—be ev'ry sentinel
This instant chang'd; the gates keep strongly
    shut.
On no pretence let any pass by them.
There's treason hatching!—But I'll search it
    out.

                      [*Exit.*

Darthula, Althan.

DARTHULA.

Conscious of what his horrid deeds deserve,
He sees th' avenging sword in ev'ry shadow.
But, anxious in suspicion, he will search.
If he discover it,—where are our hopes?

ALTHAN.

By all thy hopes and fears I must entreat
    thee,

        U u 2   To

To ſtrive ſuch apprehenſions to ſuppreſs.
For, be aſſur'd, his art will work on theſe,
And, feigning information, make thee ſpeak
In terror, what thy prudence would conceal.

DARTHULA.

He comes! The monſter!

ALTHAN.

     Labour to diſſemble
Thy ſtrong averſion.——O pretend compliance.

Enter Cairbar.

CAIRBAR, (*to himſelf.*)

'Tis certain Cathmor's not within theſe walls.
As certain 'tis he paſs'd not by the gate.
It follows then, he found ſome ſecret way,
Which none but Althan could direct him to.

ALTHAN.

Is Cathmor gone?——Would we were gone
  with him!

         His

His cruelty is now without reſtraint.

CAIRBAR.

Is this thy way, thou virtuous ſeeming
    bard!
Thou hoary hypocrite! Is this thy way?
Does it conform with that philoſophy
Profeſs'd by thee, to injure and betray
A King who gave thee life and liberty?

ALTHAN.

I thank not thee, but Cathmor for my life.
And where's the liberty thou boaſt'ſt of giv-
    ing?
Am I not ſtill thy priſoner confin'd?
When was it in my pow'r to injure thee?
Nor were it treaſon!——When did I profeſs
To be thy friend?——Yet I've befriended
    thee.
Theſe guards can vouch it; ſince you left us
    here,
I have not from Darthula's preſence ſtirr'd.
I've counſel'd her, that the moſt prudent
    ſtep
Were to be more compliable to thee.

CAIR-

CAIRBAR.

Thee and thy counfels I confide not in!
Vain are thofe arts: For I am well inform'd
Of all your plots. I know my brother's gone
To bring in Nathos by a fecret paffage!

ALTHAN.

Not long ago I faw brave Cathmor here.

CAIRBAR.

And then it was your treafons were con-
triv'd.

ALTHAN.

Canft thou fufpect of treafon that brave
    Prince,
Whofe only failing is his faithfulnefs
To fuch a brother? But if he has found
A paffage, fuch as thou imagineft,
I hope that Colla's fafe along with him.

CAIRBAR.

Ha! Colla gone?——'Tis not improbable!
                                    Let

Let Colla be this inftant here produc'd.——
You !——Carry this deceitful bard away.—
Let him be tortur'd to a full difcovery.

[*Althan led out.*

What, fair Darthula, haft thou now refolv'd?
More than the time allow'd thee is elaps'd;
And I impatient wait to hear my doom.
I hope you profited by Althan's counfel;
And find it now moft prudent to comply.

DARTHULA.

That 'tis moft prudent, all, my Lord, a-
    gree.
And were I fure that you was really chang'd,
As late you faid, to gentle and humane——
But of that change no fymptoms can I fee,
In your commanding thus a poor old bard
To be tormented, almoft in my fight.

CAIRBAR.

Kings, the moft merciful, are oft con-
    ftrain'd
To guard themfelves by fuch feverities;

And

And prudent Princes never pardon treason.

DARTHULA.

True; when their treasons are made ma-
 nifeſt.
But thus to puniſh on a bare ſuſpicion
Is liker far the tyrant than the king.

CAIRBAR.

Though fair thy perſon, fairer is thy mind!
Henceforth in virtue will I rival thee!——
Go, ſtop the tort'ring of the poor old bard!
     [*Aſide to meſſenger.*
But let him in a priſon be ſecur'd.——
Hence ſee the influence of thy pow'r on me!
Let me but know thy pleaſure, and 'tis done!
O take, and make of me whate'er thou wilt.

DARTHULA.

Thus to command a King, who governs
 many,
To my ambition is moſt flattering.
But th' approbation of a father ſtill
Is wanting to confirm me.

CAIRBAR.

Lo! he comes!
I leave thee with him.——Labour to appeafe
His juft refentment. Thou may'ft well affure
    him,
That his advice fhall all my actions fway.

(To Colla as he is entering.)

Colla, thou art a prifoner now no more.

                     [*Exit.*

Colla and Darthula.

COLLA.

My dear, dear daughter!—Do I find thee
    fafe?
No more a prifoner? What means the tyrant?
Dungeons and death were welcomer to me
Than any favours Cairbar can confer.

DARTHULA.

As foon as you was dragg'd away from us.

        X x   I

I ftill perfifting to defpife his love,
He threaten'd——'——O my father! what he
    threaten'd !——
To cut thy gray head from thy reverend
    fhoulders!——
And then by violence to——ruin me.

COLLA.

'Tis time that this old head were laid in
    duft.
But, violence!——What! Violence to thee!

DARTHULA.

One hour he only gave to think of this.
Diftracted, defperate, and perplex'd, I fought
Ev'n with my being to conclude my troubles.
Meanwhile the noble, generous Cathmor came
With foft compaffion melting in his eye,
Said that he felt my forrows, he had pledg'd
His honour for our fafe departure hence,
And would effect it, fhould it coft his life.
He's gone to bring in Nathos, by a cave
Which reaches from this caftle to the wood.
Cairbar foon mifs'd his brother. Hither he
    came,

                       With

With jealous apprehenſions agitate.
Suſpecting all our plot, he preſs'd me hard.—
I've done what thou, I fear, wilt not approve.

COLLA.

What haſt thou done?

DARTHULA.

Dear is thy life to me!

COLLA.

O my Darthula! ſee the rueful marks
Of time's deſtructive hand on this old carcaſe!
This breathing corſe, this waſted ſkeleton!
This poor incumbrance of a buſy world!
This wither'd arm behold! unſtrung its nerves,
And looſe its joints, it quivers in the breeze!
What haſt thou done for ſuch a worthleſs life?

DARTHULA.

Cathmor and Althan both advis'd me——

COLLA.

What?

X x 2

DAR-

DARTHULA.

That I, difguifing my diflike of him,
Should feign compliance, to procure delay.
I put him off with waiting your confent.
Your juft refentment, therefore, O reftrain!
And for a fhort time ufe diffimulation!

COLLA.

Diffimulation!——I deteft and loath it!—
Deceit dwells not in truly noble breafts!
That foul criterion of the groveling foul
Was ever the moft defpicable of vices;
And now by Cairbar's practice 'tis more vile!

DARTHULA.

Sufpect not that I mean to juftify
What thou condemn'ft: But fure if ever caufe
Could vindicate fuch practice, it is ours.
'Tis for our fafety indifpenfible.
'Twas ever meritorious to defeat
By any meafures fuch vile purpofes!
'Twas ever juft to turn againft our foes
Such weapons as they ufe for our deftruction.

COL-

COLLA.

In thefe old days muft I be forc'd to wield
A weapon which I never us'd in youth?
Severe neceffity !——Nor is fuccefs
From thence affur'd.——Soon will the tyrant
    come.
Didft thou not fay, that he fufpects the
    plot?
Then jealoufy will ftimulate him t' effay
If we're fincere in our intent, by urging
Th' immediate finifhing of what is fought.
In your refufal he difcovers all!
Provok'd he rages !——Cathmor is not here!
Cathmor alone reftrains his violence !——
His violence !——What will Darthula do?
My comfort is, that I fhall firft be dead.
But thou haft no alternative.

DARTHULA.

             This dagger,
This fhall at leaft preferve me from the
    worft!

                    COL-

COLLA.

'Tis what I wish'd.——Yet when propos'd
    by thee,
Thy father's tender heart almost relents,
And would diffuade thee from it!——O my
    child!
In thee are all my hopes,—and all my fears!
Be not too hafty in this defperate act!
For with thee perifh all the race of Colla!——
But perifh Colla! perifh Colla's race!
Darthula, never turn from honour's paths!

DARTHULA.

But what, my father! will become of
    thee
When I, the laft of all thy race, fhall fall?

COLLA.

Think not of me. I will not long fur-
    vive;
But in foft melancholy calmly fink,
Reflecting on my children gone before!

Ha!—See he comes!——Ye pow'rs that
    guard the good,
Protect us! Save us from this murderer!

Enter Cairbar.

CAIRBAR, *(To his soldiers as he advances.)*

'Tis past a doubt! There is a secret paf-
    fage;
And you must find it.——Make a stricter
    fearch.

(To himself.)

To stop the torturing of yon cunning bard
Was not so fafe!—From him we must extort
    it.——
They will attempt, if they are in the plot,
T' amufe me for a time with feign'd affent.
If any man out-do me in deceit,
He must have more dexterity than Colla.

                    (To

Confcious of my unworthinefs, I fear,
And tremble, while I come t' enquire my
  doom!
Forgive me, Colla!—You behold in me
An object more of pity than refentment.
For I, unhappy! I have ever been,
By blind, impetuous paffions oft impell'd
T' offend the moft, where moft I wifh'd to
  pleafe.
The injuries, the heinous injuries
So lately done to you, would I had fuffer'd!
I had not then this bitter anguifh felt.
But could my all——O could my life atone!
I'd now refign it at Darthula's feet!

DARTHULA.

Refign thy life?——Alas! Could that a-
  tone!
A life of virtue, (fuch as you propofe)
And generous actions, ufeful to mankind,
Would beft compenfate former injuries.

CAIRBAR.

'Tis true!—My death would fruftrate my
    intention
Of making an atonement more compleat,
By dedicating all my future life
To Colla's will, and fair Darthula's pleafure.
In ages yet to come fhall Erin blefs
The happy reign of Cairbar's virtuous Queen.
For thou fhalt govern me, and all my actions.
The virtuous, brought from their obfcure re-
    treats,
Shall fhine, as they deferve, with eminence.
While vice, difgrac'd, fhall fkulk in vile con-
    tempt,
Or be dragg'd out to fuffer what he merits.

COLLA.

Such kings have been in Erin!——But—
    Alas!——

CAIRBAR.

Why that Alas?——Doft thou miftruft me,
    Colla?

Y y   Ah!

Ah! Shall I never win thy confidence!

COLLA.

Believe me, Sir, I'd wiſh to ſee thee virtuous!———
But cannot now expect to—live ſo long!

CAIRBAR.

O Colla! Colla!—Wilt thou ne'er forgive
me?
Oh! canſt thou riot forget what I have done?
The thoughts of it now fill theſe eyes with
tears,
And make this breaſt, thou think'ſt ſo fierce,
to bleed!
Forget, forget it!———I will be thy ſon!
I will obey and love thee like a ſon,
And be thy future comfort of thy age.

COLLA.

A ſon of ſo much pow'r would make me
proud.
The injuries, that cannot be redreſs'd,
It is the part of prudence to forget.

CAIR-

CAIRBAR.

Thou anfwereft but in general fentences:
Thou fay'ft not yet, Darthula fhall be mine!

COLLA.

May fhe be happy in her deftin'd Lord;
Thou in thy Queen!

CAIRBAR.

　　　　　Still, ftill equivocal!
I fee their aim, and foon will difconcert it!
　　　　　　　　　　　　[*Afide.*
This unexpected happinefs quite, quite
O'erpow'rs me!——It has almoft ftruck me
　　dumb!
Darthula mine!—Come to thy lover's arms!
Thy happy, blefs'd, tranfported lover's arms!
And let us now to immediate joys retire.

COLLA.

Check thy impatience! There are previous
　　forms:
The facred, neceffary vows of love,

　　　　　　　　　　Of

Of faithful, virtuous, honourable love,
You muft fubmit to.

CAIRBAR.

Forms for fettering fools !
But be it fo, fince it is Colla's will.

(*Aloud.*)

Let all our nobles, officers, and bards,
Prepare to celebrate our inftant fpoufals,
With banqueting, with fongs, and fhouts of
joy.

DARTHULA.

Not in this caftle ! where my brother fell;
So lately fell, and fcarcely buried yet !
The laft of Colla's fons !——At this fad time
In this fad place, how could we relifh joy ? .
Grant fome few days t' extenuate our grief;
Then with becoming chearfulnefs I'll rife
To the exalted ftate of Cairbar's Queen.

CAIRBAR.

What ? for the ceremonious forms of grief
Shall

Shall I forgo fuch joys, when in my pow'r?
No! Let us timely wife, be blefs'd to day!
To-morrow will be foon enough to mourn.

DARTHULA.

Stay, I conjure thee, Cairbar! yet forbear,
Forbear a while.

CAIRBAR.

No! Bid the ocean ftop,
In midft of its career, the flowing tide!
It will obey thee fooner than my love!

DARTHULA.

It muft not be!—Not now.

CAIRBAR.

Not now?—It fhall.
Am I a king? and fhall I be controul'd?
Think ye, that I perceive not your deceit?
No rapturous wifhes tremble in your eyes;
And if your bofom beat, it is with fear,
Or hopes unfettled of your plot's fuccefs.—
I know your plots.—I know my brother's gone

To

To bring the Caledonian boy to kill me!——
That ftart confirms it all.——You have con-
    fpir'd
Againft my life; and thereby forfeit yours!
You fhall not die! But let me not repeat
My former threats.———'Tis in your pow'r to
    fhun them.

DARTHULA.

O grant me but one day! one little day!

CAIRBAR.

No!—Not a minute.   Inftantly comply;
Or—See the fword is drawn to finifh Colla.

COLLA.

Had Colla nothing worfe than death to fear,
It would not pain him: But to leave my child
At fuch a monfter's mercy, forces tears
From thefe old eyes, which have not often
    wept.

CAIRBAR.

Thy daughter's love may yet preferve thy life.

DAR¬

DARTHULA.

Thou might'ft have been belov'd, when
    thou didft feem
Humane and generous, though 'twas all af-
    fum'd:
But in this fierce, this dreadful attitude,
Thou art deteftible!

CAIRBAR.

                       I am refolv'd.
Yield thou this inftant willingly to love,
And thou fhalt be a Queen! Refufe, and fend
This fword to Colla's heart; and then expect
What force may do.

DARTHULA.

                I'll not furvive my father!—
O fpare my father! Spare that reverend head.

CAIRBAR.

Thou, thou thyfelf condemn'ft that head
    to death.
And for a kingdom wilt not ranfom it.——
                         Now

Now——But 'tis fitter for a fervile hand.
Here, guards! difpatch this traitor fpeedily.

(Shouts, warlike inftruments.)

(Soldiers flying.)

FIRST SOLDIER.

The enemy!

SECOND SOLDIER.

The enemy!

THIRD SOLDIER.

Every vault pours out frefh numbers.

Enter Nathos purfuing them off the ftage with his foldiers.

CAIRBAR.

Stand to your arms, ye flaves! Why do ye
fly?

[*Exit.*

(*As*

(As he is going, to Cathmor entring.)

Thou haft betray'd me!

CATHMOR.

       And preferv'd thee too.
'Tis now no time to ftand: The gate is open'd,
All rally on the plain beyond the caftle.

*(Shouts and warlike inftruments continued fome-
time.)*

Enter Nathos.

NATHOS.

Now is this caftle clear'd of murderers;
And not a drop of murderers blood is fhed,

CATHMOR.

Is Cairbar gone?

NATHOS.

       Aye! With the foremoft fled.

CATHMOR.

Then all is well!

         Z 2   *(Golla*

(Colla and Darthula coming forward.)

NATHOS.

If all be well with thefe ;
Docs Colla live ?—And is Darthula fafe ?

COLLA.

Yes, brave deliverers ! One minute more
Had found us weltering in our blood ! The
    fword
Was rais'd to fever this old neck ; and worfe
Than death was threaten'd to my helplefs
    child !

NATHOS.

And yet I let him pafs !

COLLA.

Let Cairbar pafs !

NATHOS.

He pafs'd within my ftroke. O how I
    burn'd
To ftrike the murderer to the favage heart !
                       But

But I had pledg'd my faith to valiant Cath-
    mor,
This generous Prince, who has preferv'd us
    all.

DARTHULA.

I cannot, gallant Prince, nor will, attempt
To fpeak my gratitude, or admiration!
I know thy foul magnanimous partakes
Of all our happinefs.

CATHMOR.

            Have I not caufe?
From the foul regifter of Cairbar's crimes
I've kept a fouler crime than any there.
I'll fight againft his enemies; his vices
I'll counteract, as his moft dangerous foes!

DARTHULA.

Oh Cathmor go not near thy murdering bro-
    ther!

CATHMOR.

My life he dares not openly affail;
And I'm aware of all his wonted arts.——

So

So much for friendſhip! Nathos, ſoon I'll
    meet thee,
An enemy in battle.——Now adieu.

        [*Exit, Nathos conveying him.*

COLLA.

How mean the conquering hero's courage
    ſeems
Compar'd with Cathmor's more exalted valour!
Greater than kings! by native virtue crown'd,
In thus defending an unworthy brother,
Who ſtands between thee and the ſovereignty!
Thou ſhow'ſt a greatneſs empires cannot give.

NATHOS, (*returning.*)

Once more muſt I, Darthula, leave thee
    here!
Cairbar collects his forces on the plain,
And ſeems determin'd to contend with ours.

COLLA.

Old as I am, infirm, and ſlow of foot,
Shall I be bound by age's fetters here!
No!—Once again I'll mount the car of battle,
And pour my vengeance on the murderers!
                There

There if I fall,—I fall as valour fhould;
Not by th' affaffin's ignominious ftab.

NATHOS.

When Colla fights, brave Colla muft com-
mand.
This day direct the war, and let me learn
From fuch a mafter, fkill'd in many a field.
I've fummon'd all the troops: We'll join them
here.

COLLA.

And I will make me ready for the field.

[*Exit.*

DARTHULA.

Muft I be left among thefe difmal fcenes
Alone to wander? flaughter raging round me!
The halls within with murder'd innocence
Polluted all !——Grim difcontented ghofts,
Yet loth to leave their limbs, will ftalk around,
Or piteous howl thro' all thefe ghaftly domes!

NATHOS.

A garrifon fufficient fhall be left

To

To man the walls, and to fecure the gates.

DARTHULA.

Stay yet, my Nathos! for my trembling
  heart
Is not yet fettled! Terror ftruck fo deep,
That wherefoe'er I turn, it ftill feems prefent.
Still I behold the tyrant's dreadful frown!
I fee the fword hang o'er my father's head !
And fhuddering feem to hear his threat'nings
  ftill !

NATHOS.

Does he pretend to love? What threaten
  thee?———
The ravenous wolf, that had not tafted food
For many a day, would rather die of famine,
Than hurt that lovely form! The foftening
  joy,
In fpite of hunger, would o'erpow'r his fierce-
  nefs,
And make him, in expiring, fawn on thee!

DARTHULA.

What if my Nathos muft return no more?
                              And

And my poor father in the battle fall?
Then Cairbar comes victorious!—Dreadful
    thought!
None to defend me from his cruelty!

NATHOS.

If we should fall, to my old father fly:
Our ships are ready to convey thee thither.

DARTHULA.

To live without thee were the worst of
    deaths!
To die with thee were joy! Our ghosts toge-
    ther
Shall unmolested wander o'er the plain,
Skim the smooth surface of the summer lake,
Or on the clouds above the mountains fly.
We'll ride upon the whirlwind's rapid wings,
And sink the ships where murdering Cairbars
    fail.

NATHOS.

We may yet long be blest in life and love.
At my return you'll ask how Cairbar fell.
And long, long after this, our tears shall flow
When gladly we relate these dangers past,
               And

And make our children tremble with the tale.

[A trumpet.

I muſt begone!—Farewell! I'll ſee thee ſoon.

DARTHULA, (*alone.*)

If e'er I ſee thee, 'tis beyond my hopes:
For awful ſhadows of approaching woe,
Still deeply-darkening, on my fancy glide.
What dire diſaſters have this day befallen us!
Do more await us? Ravens and eagles ſoar
Above their heads! Do theſe foul birds of prey
Mark out the bodies which they long to tear?
The dreadful gleaming of their weapons ſeems
Like that ill-boding flame that flies along
The way, where ſoon the funeral ſhall paſs.—
Am I deceiv'd?——Do I not ſee the ghoſts
Of all my brothers bending from their clouds,
And beckoning Colla hence?——
What ſhrieks were theſe?——What's that?—
 my father here?
All wounds! all blood! now pale! now black
 as earth!
Was it th'illuſion of a frighted fancy?
No! 'twas the harbinger of certain death.

END OF THE THIRD ACT.

CHORUS

CHORUS III.

Scene in Sight of the Field of Battle.

Carril and other Bards.

CARRIL.

Come, Bards, in thoughts and numbers free,
  Unfetter'd all with fruitlefs flow'rs,
Sing what we of the fight fhall fee,
  As prompted by the tuneful pow'rs.

SECOND BARD.

In nature's bold, but ready ftrains
  Let the unmeafur'd numbers flow,
Varying with the various fcenes,
  That war fhall now prefent of blifs or woe.

CHORUS.

Come, Bards, in numbers bold and free,
Prepare to fing the fcenes we fee!

THIRD

THIRD BARD.

Collecting death, on either hand,
In awful paufe both armies ftand,
Like two oppofing clouds that lowr
Ready to difcharge their wrath,
In rain, or hail's impetuous fhow'r,
The thunder's rough tremenduous roar,
And flafh that fudden ftrikes with death.

FOURTH BARD.

Already the declining beams
    Saffron o'er the weftern fkies ;
Gray mifts from the running ftreams,
    From the lakes and marfhes rife.

CARRIL.

Gray mifts to mortals thefe appear !
    But, mortals, could ye fee aright,
Ghofts of warriors mufter there,
    To behold the important fight.

CHORUS.

Glide flow, great ghofts, along the vale !
    Or, hovering o'er their heads, behold
                       Your

Your fons confirm each wond'rous tale,
That ancient bards of you have told.

FIFTH BARD.

Colla to the deftin'd field
Drives his lofty car.

B. 6. Now he ftrikes his founding fhield!

B. 7. Now, now begins the war.

B. 8. Both armies advancing with ardour engage.

B. 9. The Demon of Battle has loos'd all his
rage.

B. 10. Stones, arrows, and javelins, darken the
fky!

B. 11. Some wounded already are falling behind!

B. 12. In vain they look forward! Their weaknefs they find.

All. But whence comes that forrowful cry?

B. 13. 'Twas from our own hoft!

B. 14. Some hero we've loft.

B. 15. 'Tis Althos that falls to the ground.

All. A hero we've loft:
'Tis Althos that lies on the ground!

Car. I'll view the nature of his wound.

Chor. Ill-fated victim of the noble flame
Deftructive only to the brave!

A a a 2   How

How many youths, like thee, purfuing
  fame,
  Have drop'd into a grave?
Yet Bards thy fame fhall raife:
  For having feen
Thy manhood in thy early days,
They'll guefs what thou mature hadft
  been,
  And fing thy praife.

B. 1. In fury the combatants clofe,
  With fword againft fword, and fpear a-
    gainft fpear.
B. 2. With pufhes and blows they each other
    oppofe,
  All aiming deftruction and death at
    their foes.
B. 3. What havoc! What flaughter! now yon-
    der, now here.
B. 4.   From the bloody ftreams,
      The fun's declining beams
      Rebound in horrid gleams;
B. 5. And through blood all the features of
    nature appear!
B. 6. Rank drives on rank.

B. 7.

B. 7.   They fall, they die.

B. 8. Their friends behold without a figh!

B. 9. On heaps of flaughter rifing high,
      They fill the dangerous place.

B. 10. But foon, too foon, alas!
      Thofe warriors in thofe heaps may ly.

B. 11.   Behold upon our right,
          Where Nathos leads the fight;
          Like a river fwell'd with rain,
          That burfts the bounding banks,
          He breaks thro' hoftile ranks.

B. 12. Thofe ranks give way!

B. 13.   They take to flight!

B. 14.   All fcatter'd o'er the plain,
      They fall at ev'ry blow!

Chor. Rufh on! Strike home, till all be flain.
      End the war, and end our woe!

B. 15. Our left in confufion!

All.   They fly, they fly!
      Fall not in diforder! Recover the line!

B. 16. Who makes all this havoc?

B. 17. What warrior is he?

All. 'Tis Cathmor himfelf, or fome fpirit
      divine.

Chor. Ceafe, friend of men! from flaughter ceafe!
      Can Cathmor be a cruel foe?

                              Thou

Thou life, thou joy of all in peace!
    Canſt thou in war bring death and woe?

B. 1.   · Colla, in his lofty car,
      Leading on a choſen band,
      Ruſhes boldly through the war,
To ſuccour the flying.

B. 2.   They rally!

B. 3.   They ſtand!

B. 4. They charge with new vigour again.

B. 5.   They cover the plain
      With heaps newly ſlain!

All. They are proud to fight under brave
      Colla's command.

B. 6. Cathmor far from Colla keep;
      Unequal is the ſtrife!

B. 7. Even thy own gallant heart would weep
    . For ending ſuch a life.

B. 8. But Colla turn where late you led;
      The main has now your abſence found.

B. 9. With equal fate, while you was at their
        head,
    They fought and bled.
    But now they're loſing ground.

B. 10. Faint and languid falls each ſtroke.

B. 11. Support them, or they'll ſoon be broke.

                         B. 12.

B. 12. Is there no chief to chear?

B. 13. No fuccours near?

Chor. Difmal is the face our fortunes wear.

B. 14. But who comes over the height?

B. 15. Impatience appears in his ftride.

B. 1.   Already at the fight

    With fpirit now they fight.

B. 2. Th' advantage appears on their fide.

B. 3. 'Tis he that wields Cuchullin's fpear.

B. 4. And who wields that, but Ufnoth's

    fon?

B. 5. Conqueft he over their left has won.

B. 6. He charges their main in flank and

    rear.

B. 7.   New courage returning,

    With new fury burning,

 Our friends lately fainting fight fiercely

    again.

B. 8.   While the foe all furrounded,

    Diforder'd, confounded,

    On every fide wounded,

    By hundreds are flain.

Chor. Difmay and terror, havoc, horror,

   Urging on their hurried flight;

   Crying, flying, groaning, dying,

   No hopes but in th' approaching night.

          B. 9.

B. 9.   Cathmor, ever truly great,
    Unchang'd by ev'ry change of fate,
    Draws off his conquering troops, to
        cover the retreat.

B. 10.   Backward he flowly goes,
    Intrepid in the rear,
    Calmly repelling his purfuing foes.

B. 11. Victorious fquadrons from his blows
    Recoil with fear.

Chor. Powers benign! may never dart
    Strike him in a mortal part!
    Guard, O guard that generous heart,
    Which ev'n his foes revere!

CARRIL.

No longer fing!——'Tis time to fearch the
    field,
For wounded friends, who lying there in
    pain,
Long for th' affiftance of our healing art.

           [*Exeunt all but Carril.*

A C T

A C T IV.

Scene continues.——The Evening.

CARRIL, (*alone.*)

Is my old fight deceiv'd by evening's dufk?
Or is it Colla comes fupported thus?

Enter Colla, carried by foldiers.

COLLA.

Now ftop, my friends! Here fet me foftly
    down!——
Fain would I fee my daughter ere I die;
But find, this motion rankles fo my wound,
That I fhould die before I reach'd the caftle.

CARRIL.

Let lights be brought t' examine Colla's
    wound.

B b b   COL-

COLLA.

No matter, Carril, what becomes of me!
Your fkill may be more ufefully employed:
Here many vigorous lives you may preferve.

CARRIL.

Can I not yet preferve the life of Colla?

COLLA.

You fee how deep this arrow lodges here!
With this my foul will iffue forth, to greet
The mighty fpirits in our fongs renown'd.

CARRIL.

The wound is mortal!

COLLA.

Short while it prevents
The flow, but certain fap of wafting age!
Which every day was gaining on my vitals.

CARRIL.

Ah you had ftrength to hold out many
years!

COL-

COLLA.

I might have dragg'd with pain an uſeleſs
  life,
For a few tedious melancholy years!
No joys had I in life!—Is this not better?—
Oh had I found the vengeance which I ſought!
And ſeen my child by Cairbar's death ſecure,
In cloſing theſe old eyes I had rejoic'd,
To die a ſoldier of unſpotted fame!

CARRIL.

If thou would'ſt ſee thy daughter, O ſup-
  preſs
Paſſion's inflammatory virulence,
Which haſtens on thy few remaining minutes.

Enter Darthula and Althan.

(With Ladies and ſoldiers attending.)

DARTHULA.

Is that not he ſo pale by yonder light!——
And

And art thou dead before I could receive
Thy laſt ſad counſel from thy dying lips?

COLLA.

No, my Darthula! ſtill thy father lives!
He wiſh'd to live till now, that he beholds
The ſole ſurviving object of his care!

DARTHULA.

O Carril! Althan! Can ye not preſerve
So dear a life?

CARRIL AND ALTHAN.

'Tis paſt the pow'r of art.

DARTHULA.

Why do ye weep?——Ye have no cauſe to
weep!——
Leave that to me!—For I was born to mourn.

COLLA.

Weep not for me.——Thy ſorrows, O my
child,
Give me more pain than does this outward
wound.

DAR-

DARTHULA.

Shall I not weep? Shall I not weep for
    thee?
For thee, my father? I alone am left
Of all thy race? Shall I not mourn thy fall?

COLLA.

Yes! thou of all my race art left alone.——
That race, I hope, may yet revive in thee,
Though I shall never see it.——But the pain,
That more I feel than all my dying pangs,
Proceeds from leaving thee so unsecure.
If thou wert safe beyond this murderer's
    reach,
I'd go with pleasure to embrace the shades
Of all my family now waiting round me.

DARTHULA.

If to be murder'd were the worst I fear'd,
I would not grieve.——In transports could I
    go
Along with thee to join that happy group!
But who shall aid, protect, or counsel me,
                         When

When thou art gone? Advife me what to do,
Whilft yet thou canft advife me! That ad-
    vice
Shall with my father's image ever be
My bofom's deareft treasure.

COLLA.

                    Fly from hence!
Here Cairbar is; and here are many fuch
Of fordid, felfifh, avaricious fouls,
Who will by falfehood, ftratagem, or force,
Attempt thy perfon for the large domains
That now unhappily devolve to thee.——
Seek thy protection in a hufband's arms!——
May he be loving, faithful, generous, brave!
Such Nathos is.——In him thou mayft con-
    fide.——
With him to Caledonia quickly fly!——
May you be happy there!——O may the race
Of old Selama fpring afrefh from you!——

DARTHULA.

Where, where is he? Have not his wounds
    increas'd
The dreadful deluge of this bloody field?

CARRIL.

· I hear his voice! He comes from the purfuit.

NATHOS, (*entering.*)

Though ev'ry where with ardour him I
    fought,
He no lefs anxioufly avoided me:
And when his army broke, this boafting chief,
This king of flaughter, with the foremoft
    fled.———
Cathmor, who nobly fell into their rear
And there with valour to be envy'd fought,
Reftrain'd the progrefs of our firft purfuit;
Elfe had I fwam the flood, and climb'd the
    mountain,
Chac'd him along the narrow precipice,
Under the danger of the falling rocks,
And to the whirlwind giv'n his howling
    ghoft.

DARTHULA.

O Nathos! Nathos! Colla is no more!

NATHOS.

NATHOS.

Alas, the good old chieftain! who so oft
Brought honour's brighteſt wreaths from
    danger's field!
Who has in this his lateſt day diſplay'd
A valour that made youth to wiſh for years!
Sedate and temperate in the hotteſt ſtrife,
He brought to my remembrance what I had
    heard
Of that great Pow'r, which rides above the
    ſtorm,
Conducting calmly its deſtructive courſe!
And art thou gone?——

COLLA.

Am going faſt, my Nathos!

NATHOS.

He ſpeaks!—He knows me!—How is it
    with Colla?

COLLA.

As with a ſoldier who has ſtruggled long
                 With

With all the hardſhips of a diſtant war,
When from the neareſt height he kens his
    home.

NATHOS.

O victory too dear, that is acquir'd
With ſo much precious blood!

COLLA.

               Too much indeed!
My life is nothing!——It is more than ripe!
But many blooming youths, with both thy
    brothers,
Are in the bloſſom of their vigour crop'd!

NATHOS.

   What both my brothers! Ardan I ſaw fall.
Ah! how fell Althos?

COLLA.

           As the brave ſhould fall.
He too impetuous haſted to the foe.——
The hoſtile archers mark'd his goodly mien.
His manly valour with the danger grew!—
While yet I look'd at him, an arrow came,

         C c c   And

And to the feather in his bosom sunk.———
I strove to hide my grief———I felt his death,
As if another son of mine had fallen.———

NATHOS.

Shall my poor brothers never more return
To fill their aged father's heart with joy?
But joy no more shall fill my father's heart:
For never, never shall his sons return!

COLLA.

Usnoth has yet one worthy son in thee!—
O my Darthula! soon thou'lt have no father!—
Thou hast no brother to protect thee now!—

NATHOS.

If I am worthy, think thou leav'st in me
A son, who shall revere thy memory!
Who all the affection of a father, join'd
To that of many brothers, shall exceed,
For this dear maid; and with more zeal pro-
  tect her.

COLLA.

I'm satisfy'd, my son!—Be kind to her!———

DAR-

DARTHULA.

Alas! alas!—How weak thou grow'ſt, my
father!

COLLA.

Oh! Bear me to the tent! Farewell my Nathos!——
Now all that I poſſeſs'd is thine!

NATHOS.

Of that
Darthula is by far the deareſt part!
[*Colla carried out, Darthula, Carril, Al-
than following.*

NATHOS, (*alone.*)

Like Colla let me live! like Colla die!
Like him by every ſtep move to renown!
Not fade in ſpirit when my limbs decay,
But bravely meet, in arms, the ſword of
death.

Enter

Enter Usnoth attended.

USNOTH.

My Nathos!

NATHOS.

Ha!—My father come to Erin?

USNOTH.

Thy victory was the firſt happy news
That I heard utter'd on th' Erinian ſhore!
It makes thy aged father's heart exult
To ſee this riſing ſun of thy renown!

NATHOS.

Why has my father, in his hoary days,
Reſum'd the buckler, which he had reſign'd
To ruſt with thoſe of his great anceſtors.

USNOTH.

Since firſt we heard of brave Cuchullin's
    death,

Dire

Dire apprehenfions have thy father t**rn** !
'Tis faid no fenfe of honour e'er reftrain'd
The cruel Cairbar from ungenerous plots :
That he, deceitful, waits in çonftant am-
    bufh
To feize th' advantage of unguarded hours.
My arm, indeed, is now of fmall avail !
But I am old, and you are young in arms !

NATHOS.

What army haft thou brought?

USNOTH.

        Our force is great.
Fingal·has fent before his chofen youths,
Conducted by his grandfon valiant Ofcar.
Himfelf is following with a greater force
Of veteran troops, t' avenge the death of Cor-
    mac.

NATHOS.

And where is Ofcar?

USNOTH.

      Landing now his troops
                    In

In Tura's bay. The ship that carried me,
Complying with th' impatience of my wishes,
Outsail'd the rest, and hurried me to joy.

NATHOS.

My good old father!

USNOTH.

Ha!—Where are your brothers?

NATHOS.

Alas! my father!——They in battle fell.

USNOTH.

What! Both my younger boys? You said
not both!

NATHOS.

But both are slain.——And here old Colla
too!——

USNOTH.

What! Colla too?—My friend! and both
my sons!

NATHOS.

Be comforted, my father!

USNOTH.

O, my Nathos!——
I am the father now of none but thee!

NATHOS.

They fought like heroes!——They have
fall'n renown'd!

USNOTH.

I hope they have!——But many glorious
years
They might have fought, exalting their re-
nown!——
I, too indulgent to th' infatuate pray'rs
Of youth precipitate, fent them to meet,
Ere they had ftrength t' encounter, danger's
grafp!

NATHOS.

Their valour merited a better fate!

USNOTH.

How fudden chang'd to mourning are the
 joys
I felt at my firft landing on this coaft!——
Among the flaughter'd bodies twice I ftum-
 bled!
In one I thought I faw my Ardan's fhapes!
Evening obfcur'd the face!——I chid my
 heart
For fuch a dire fuggeftion!——O, twas he!

ALTHAN, (*entering.*)

Colla's great fpirit is at laft at peace!
Darthula pours her pious forrow forth
Upon the breathlefs body.

USNOTH.

   O my friend!——

NATHOS.

My father, you muft fee this beauteous
 maid!
Not more for beauty than for prudence fam'd,
And ev'ry female virtue!——She alone
      Survives

Survives of Colla's lately numerous race.
To me her father's dying breath bequeath'd
    her;
And ties of mutual love unite our hearts.

USNOTH.

'Tis now no time t'intrude upon her for-
    rows.

Enter Dermid.

DERMID.

Short way has Cairbar fled! We fee their
    fires
Now blazing on the height beyond the heath.

NATHOS.

To-morrow we'll diflodge him.

DERMID.

           Has our chief,
'The ever-honour'd Ufnoth brought an army?

USNOTH.

A little army, Dermid, we have landed.
        D d d   But

But Fingal, Morven's never-conquer'd King,
Who, vigorous still, with locks as white as
  mine,
Makes youthful fquadrons fly before his
  fword,
Is landing now with a much greater force.

DERMID.

Moft grateful tidings!——For we now fuf-
  pect
Some fecret treafon in th' Erinian troops.
In bufy whifpers, cautioufly remov'd
From Caledonian ears, their chiefs confer.

NATHOS.

'Tis not improbable: Their King is flain,
And Colla dead. Perhaps they grudge t'obey
A foreigner's commands, and now confpire
To rob me of my pow'r.

DERMID.

      'Tis that we fear.

NATHOS.

Keep you ftrict watch to-night.
        DERMID.

DERMID.

Moſt needful 'tis !

[*Exit.*

NATHOS.

I have of late obſerv'd a diſcontent
Among the veteran chiefs. Should they re-
volt,
Our force is nothing. Few our native troops:
And ev'n of thoſe the better part was left
To garriſon the caſtle of Temora.
Could not your army join with ours to-night?

USNOTH.

I will endeavour it. My chariot waits.
I'll go to Oſcar, and will bring them hither
With all the ſpeed I can. Meanwhile fare-
well. [*Exit.*

NATHOS.

Thy being here, alas, my good old father!
Is an addition to my former cares.

D d d 2

Enter

Enter Darthula.

DARTHULA.

Woe ftill fucceeds to woe: And forrows have
Mark'd ev'ry period of Darthula's life !
At haplefs Fruthil's birth my mother dy'd !
One after one my gallant brothers fell !
The laft this morning !—And my father now !
My dear, dear father !—Shall thy words no more
Appeafe my forrows, diffipate my fears,
And ftrengthen ev'ry virtue in my breaft ?

NATHOS.

Mourn not for Colla !——He has but ex-
chang'd
A life of forrow for a life of blifs.
A life he wifh'd for, of immortal youth,
With all his family rejoicing round !——
The only anguifh now they feel, is that
A daughter's and a fifter's forrow gives.

DARTHULA.

I know he's happy ! Know his prefence brings
Increafe.

Increaſe of pleaſure to the realms of joy!—
But how can we, who have that preſence loſt,
Not feel our loſs?——Long muſt I mourn for
   him!

NATHOS.

Now deep theſe griefs are on our minds
   impreſs'd;
But time, that wears the titles from their
   tombs,
Will wear theſe deep impreſſions from our
   minds,
And ſmooth them to receive ſucceeding joy.
Some of our deareſt friends are ſnatch'd away:
But thou art left; and that ſhall comfort me!

DARTHULA.

Yes, I am left! And ſo the lamb is left
That weary ſlaughter till to-morrow ſpares!
Do ye, indeed, dear ſhades! partake our ſor-
   rows?
Then ye perceive and feel our dangers too!—
Our danger's great! The murderer ſtill exiſts,
To form new ſtratagems for our deſtruction!
O fly, my Nathos, from this dangerous land:
For ſafety is not in it!——Fly from Cairbar.
                             N A-

NATHOS.

What! Shall we leave the field of victory,
And all our honour to a vanquifh'd foe?
No! here we'll watch all night upon our arms,
To catch the firft glimpfe of the morning's
      beams.
Then, then; thou tyrant, I will be reveng'd
For all the precious lives thou haft deftroy'd.

DARTHULA.

There are more lives! there are more pre-
      cious lives,
That he will ever labour to deftroy.
And I, my Nathos, hazard more than life!—
I have no friend, no kindred to defend me;
No hopes have I of fafety but in thee;
Nor ev'n with thee have hopes of fafety here!

NATHOS.

In thy defence what would I not attempt?
I'd rufh between thee and a falling rock!
I'd catch a thunder-bolt that threaten'd thee!
What would'ft thou have me do?

DARTHULA.

      Alas! what caufe
           Have

Have we to ſtay in this now-waſted land ?
It was my father's laſt advice to leave it
As ſoon as poſſible !——See all around,
How ev'ry circumſtance ev'n now concurs
With that my prudent father's laſt advice !——
No ray of ev'ning bluſhes in the weſt;
But night's dark ſhades have with th' horizon
      clos'd,
To hide our embarkation from the foe :
While night's fair Queen now riſes from the
      waves,
With duſky light to guide us through the
      gloom !
No angry ſtorm frowns on the diſtant hill,
Portentous to the fearful mariner :
But weſtern breezes, ruſtling o'er the rocks,
Make the gay glittering moon-beams ſportive
      play
Upon the curling ſurface of the main,
And will convey us quick to Etha's ſhore !

NATHOS.

Thy ſweet words make ev'n cowardice ſeem
      fair !
But let us hazard here this one ſhort night,
                   And

And wait the burying of our friends to-mor-
    row.
And we have friends that yet thou know'ft
    not of.
My father now was here! He brings with
    him
A powerful army, fent by Morven's King
To ftrengthen us.

DARTHULA.

       Ha! that brings hopes indeed!
And gives me comfort in the midft of woe!

NATHOS.

Ha! What means this?——There's an un-
    ufual buftle
Among our troops.   I'll fee what it imports.
                    [*Exit.*

DARTHULA, (*alone.*)

Haft thou already reach'd the aerial feats
Of happy fouls? Or doft thou mournful here
Behold my tears with fympathizing woe?——
Could I forget thee, and indulge the hopes
The prefent profpect of my fate affords,
                    Thou

Thou would'ft depart to blifs without a figh!
Go then, dear fpirit! let my brothers know,
That Cairbar flies; that the felected force.
Of Morven's never-conquer'd heroes comes
To perfect conqueft, and enfure our joy.

Enter Nathos with feveral officers.

NATHOS.

Hafte, Ronan, hafte, with all thy wonted
  fpeed!
Tell them that they muft come immediately,
With all the troops they've landed: For we
  ftand
Between two armies. Each too potent far
For our diminifh'd force.

DARTHULA.

Ah! what means this?

NATHOS.

Great, my Darthula, is our danger now!
For our Erinians in a body march
To fight againft us on the adverfe fide!

DARTHULA.

What! All th' Erinians?

ONE OF COLLA'S OFFICERS.

No, Darthula, no!
Thy father's friends are faithful ſtill to thee;
And will defend thee while their lives remain:
For ſo they bid me tell thee.

DARTHULA.

And their friendſhip
I will remember while my life remains.
But though they're brave, though brave the
    Caledonians,
Hardy in toil, and faithful to their chief,
Strong and reſiſtleſs as the impetuous torrents
That, ſwell'd with rain, ruſh down their native
    hills;
Yet what can they, ſo few, againſt ſo many?
O Nathos, is there yet no way to fly?

NATHOS.

I fear there is not: for they eaſtward move
Between us and our friends upon the ſhore;
               Between

Between us and the caftle. If they pafs it,
We will make it our refuge till to-morrow.

OFFICER.

But be affur'd they will not pafs it now;
For this is plainly their concerted plan,
To cut us off. They dar'd us, as they went,
To follow them; which if we 'ad rafhly done,
Cairbar was ready to attack our rear.

DARTHULA.

Are there no hopes?——May we not yet
    efcape them?

NATHOS.

Go, Dermid, to the north, and, Connel,
    fouth:
Try if we could not pafs them there unfeen.
Meanwhile, hard by there is an eminence,
On one fide bounded by a wall of rocks;
There we'll prepare ourfelves, the beft we can,
For our defence, if we fhould be attack'd.

                   [*Exeunt.*

END OF THE FOURTH ACT.

        CHORUS

C H O R U S IV.

SCENE, *The fea-fhore. The army landing by moon-light.*

BARDS AND SOLDIERS.

FIRST BARD.

GLIDE on, fair fplendid Queen of night,
　Through yon ferene and fable fky !
White-fkirted clouds; blaze all with light !
　Darknefs, beyond the mountains fly !
　　Ye winds, your breath reftrain !
　　Thou palely-fhining main,
　　　Still all thy fwelling waves !
Ye Ghofts, who with malicious joy
Mifguided mariners annoy,
　　　Reft in your hollow caves !
Come, fathers, brothers, children, whom
　We loft, when lately here before !
Your fame we fung ! We rais'd your tombs !
　The lofs of you we ftill deplore !
With good-portending omens come,
　　And welcome us afhore !

　　　　　　　　　　　　　Enter

Enter Soldiers.

SOLDIERS.

Huzza! Huzza! Huzza!

SECOND SOLDIER.

Come on, my brave fellows! Well known is
  this ground;
Well known ev'ry object before ye;
'Tis here that our valour by deeds is renown'd,
  And eſtabliſh'd forever our glory.
'Twas but the laſt year in this harbour we
  landed;
By our preſent brave leaders we then were
  commanded.
  So hot on yon plain,
  We handled the Dane,
That Swaran was bound, his fierce warriors
  were ſlain;
And the war by one battle was ended.

SOLDIERS.

Huzza! Huzza! Huzza!
And the war by, &c.

THIRD

THIRD SOLDIER.

Incited by nobleſt ambition we go
  Where honour and glory invite us!
The more we're oppos'd, the more ardent we
     grow;
  No labours, no dangers affright us!
But O the delight! when returning with glory,
Your friends crowd around ye: your ladies
     adore ye!
    They fly to your arms ;——
    Then bleſt in their charms,
You talk of paſt dangers, of hardſhips, alarms;
  And hear their ſongs echo your ſtory!

SOLDIERS.

  Huzza! Huzza! Huzza!
  And hear their ſongs, &c.

FOURTH SOLDIER.

Glimmering in the moon's pale light,
Yonder ſtones of diſmal white
Mournful mark the places where,
    With many a tear,
    Our friends we laid.

                  Some

Some of us too muſt lie there.
But be not diſmay'd:
In Swaran's war, though many fell,
Yet many more were left to tell,
How they with honour fought;
And how they fell, as ſoldiers ought.
Inevitable fate.
Awaits us all!
But come it ſoon, or come it late,
Like them renown'd we'll fall.

FIFTH SOLDIER.

In hall ſuperb, or hamlet-hut,
When with the ſhell the ſong goes round,
Our children yet unborn ſhall ſilent ſit,
And hear the bards our praiſe reſound.
The ever-animating rhimes
Succeeding bards ſhall learn from them!
Soldiers of long diſtant times,
Shall from our valour catch the noble flame.
When ſpirits, hovering near,
With raptures we ſhall hear
Our children's lateſt offspring ſing our fame.
Die ſoon, die late, our ſpirits live
In joys more pure than ſenſe can give.

SIXTH SOLDIER.

But you that safe return from war
   Your miſtreſs meets with open arms !
With pride ſhe'll mark each graceful ſcar
   That heightens all your manly charms.
Then, then ye warriors, lay aſide
The ſoldier's frown, the ſoldier's pride !
Soft and ſoothing are th' alarms
That ſound the charge to beauty's arms.

SEVENTH SOLDIER.

  He plays a fooliſh game
  Who hazards life for fame,
  And on that fame relies
  T' inſpire love's flame.
For ſhould the loſs of limbs or eyes,
  His ſtrength or beauty maim,
The ladies would the fool deſpiſe
  With all his boaſted fame.
We've ſeen, while in the bloody field,
The ſoldier made his thouſands yield,
By ſome gay youth in love more ſkill'd,
The hero's miſtreſs from him torn !
How, ſoldier, how ſhall this be borne?
Better

Better with steel hadst thou been kill'd,
Than with a woman's scorn!

EIGHTH SOLDIER.

Away, silly fopling! How vainly ye rave!
To think that such dunces as you,
Will e'er by the fair be esteem'd like the brave,
With victory's wreaths on his brow!
Such painted moth-flies
The ladies despise;
Though rolling your eyes,
Though heaving soft sighs,
Ye think ye are wonderous charming!
Though smiling most sweetly, though looking
so wise,
Though frisking and lisping out ignorant lies,
The conduct of soldiers ye dare criticise,
And of battles and sieges determine!
A soldier who wants both his limbs and his
eyes,
Is worth twenty tribes of such vermin.

ACT

ACT V.

Scene, An open field.

DARTHULA, *(alone.)*

AND now, though 'twas our wish, we could
    not fly.——
The moon-light face of heav'n, erewhile so
    calm,
And seemingly inviting, now is chang'd
To gloomy darkness, and loud-howling storms.
Instead of soft West-winds, the boisterous east
Lets loose his roughest blasts: All nature feels
The dreadful uproar blustering through her
    works,
And trembles lest her spacious empire fall.
The shatter'd forest groans, the mountains
    shake,
And like continued thunder roar the waves.
How terrible to those who are surpriz'd
Amidst their horrors! Dreadful too to me!
Tho' forc'd to fly we could not now escape.
So strong the billows break upon the beach,
That to encounter them were certain death.
                          But

But death in any shape is better far
Than here to meet the tyrant's cruelties.

NATHOS, (*entering in haste.*)

Where is Darthula? All is lost, my love!
Our treacherous Erinians have deserted,
And join'd the tyrant's troops; our trusty
    friends,
The Caledonian troops, befet at once,
O'erpow'r'd by multitudes, e'er yet awake,
Are either slain, or prisoners to Cairbar.

DARTHULA.

O Nathos is there no way to escape?

NATHOS.

Dost thou not hear how furious tempests rage?
Dost thou not hear the billows how they roar,
As if they'd burst the barriers of their strength,
And tofs the massy rocks, like froth, in air?
Bare is the rugged bottom in their hollows;
While scarce a passage for our ships is left
Betwixt their lofty ridges and the stars.
And, like a circling wall, the troops of Cairbar
Incompass us around.—What shall we do?
I might indeed rush on their crowded spears,

    And

And make with honour my retreat from life.
But what becomes of thee?

DARTHULA.

     I will not live!
Death is the danger which I fear the leaft!

NATHOS.

Come death or life, I will remain with thee!
Farewell, farewell to all the dear, dear hopes
Of mutual love, which flatter'd us fo lately!
Now all our hopes are here to die together!

DARTHULA.

O Nathos!—Doft thou love me?

NATHOS.

    Why that queftion?

DARTHULA.

Then fend my foul before to wait on thine,
Among the fpirits of our friends departed!—

NATHOS.

Shocking to thought! Think'ft thou I could
  do this?

        DAR-

DARTHULA.

And wilt thou let me live to meet the ty-
 rant,
With all his paffions heighten'd by fuccefs?
Send, Nathos, fend my foul beyond his
  pow'r!——
I will not mingle with the happy fhades,
Till Nathos come!—I'll hover o'er thy head!
I'll ftrive to turn their weapons from thy
  heart!——
Their wounds fhall firft transfix my airy
  form!——
When thy dear foul comes forth, we'll fmil-
  ing clafp,
And in each others arms foar to the ftars.

NATHOS.

More favage ev'n than Cairbar would he
 be,
Who could deftroy that form of lovelinefs!

DARTHULA.

No toils, no dangers but thou would'ft encounter,
        With

With pleasure, to deliver me from death.——
With worse, far worse than death, I'm now
    beset!——
'Tis in thy pow'r with ease to rescue me!——
Ev'n with one little stroke!—Is that refus'd?

NATHOS.

Shall Nathos kill Darthula? Never, never!
One stroke at Cairbar's heart! That, that
    would save thee!

DARTHULA.

Such safety would be foolish to expect!——
Ah! if thou canst not strike, hold here the
    sword!
To avoid him I will run upon its point.
Death, which we think so dreadful, soon is
    past!
Soon, soon our spirits shall assume new forms,
Perhaps more lovely, better form'd for joy,
And proof against all life's distressing fears!

NATHOS.

If death be such, it is not to be fear'd,
But rather wish'd for!

DAR-

DARTHULA.

Now he comes! he comes!—
I have no hopes, no refuge but in death!—
O Nathos! wilt thou not assist me there?

NATHOS.

That desperate remedy must be the last!

DARTHULA.

'Tis time t' apply that remedy!——He's
here!——
And if thou wilt not, here's a dagger will!—

NATHOS, (*taking the dagger.*)

Forbear, forbear, let me not see thee dead.

Enter Cairbar behind a strong party of spearmen.

CAIRBAR.

Halt! And advance not till you are com-
manded.
Darthula! now thy Nathos stands at bay!
He cannot save thee, or defend himself
From

From inftant death againft fo many fpears!

NATHOS.

—Yes, murderer; I expect no lefs than death,
When in thy pow'r!—To-day thou waft in
    mine.
I offer'd thee an equal combat then;
But thou com'ft like a frighted hedge-hog
    now,
Shrunk up within thy prickles. Forward
    come
Into the front, and pour thy vengeance forth.

CAIRBAR.

Shall I, who conquer kingdoms, and de-
    fcend
Of mighty kings, contend on equal terms
With thee, a boy unknown to fame, and
    fprung
From fubject parents of a fmall renown?

NATHOS.

Th' excufe is worthy of thy little foul!
Thou dar'ft not fight. The cruel ne'er were
    brave.

On

On equal terms!—Thefe I demanded not.
Thefe I expect not.——If thou dar'ft, come
    forward
To danger's front, where leaders ought to be,
I'll fight againft thee with this dreadful odds.

CAIRBAR.

I take no counfel of fuch things as thee.
But, that this Lady may not think me cruel,
Though fometimes forc'd by blood t' affert
    my right,
And as I make of thee but fmall account,
I fend thee to thy father fafely home.

NATHOS.

On what conditions doft thou offer this?

CAIRBAR.

Conditions! None will I demand of thee!
But thou, fair captive, now become my own
By right of conqueft, muft with me remain!
Would'ft thou do much to fave a lover's life?
That life fo dear thou may'ft with eafe pre-
    ferve.——
If thou with feeming willingnefs confent
To be my Queen, I now difmifs him fafe.

G g g   NA-

NATHOS.

I value not my life at such a rate.

DARTHULA.

Who can confide in treaties made with Cairbar ?

CAIRBAR.

Think how absurd in thee 'tis to refuse
What thou art so unable to withhold!
I only ask, for form's sake, thy consent
To what I can, and am resolv'd to effect,
Whether 'tis given or no.———Since 'tis re-
fus'd,
This instant dies thy lover ; and thyself,
On terms to thee by much less honourable,
Shalt be compell'd t' obedience of my will.

DARTHULA.

I'll die with him ! but shall not live with
thee !

CAIRBAR.

Then all advance upon him.

NATHOS, (*putting himself in a posture of defence.*)

I am ready!

DAR-

DARTHULA, (*running before him.*).

Through me! through me, your fpears muft
  reach his heart !

CAIRBAR.

Defpis'd ! infulted ! I will be reveng'd!
I'll bind thee faft, thou mad prefumptuous
    boy !
And in thy fight enjoy this haughty maid,
Who dares for thee reject an offer'd kingdom.

NATHOS.

In that, vile murderer, I defy thy pow'r!
Never alive fhall I come in thy hands !
I am refolv'd upon a defperate death !
Many fhall bleed around me ere I fall !

CAIRBAR.

Secure the Lady firft.

NATHOS.

        Stand off, ye flaves !
'Tis death to ev'ry ruffian that attempts it.

CAIRBAR.

Come up behind him.

CAR-

DARTHULA, (*going behind is seized.*)

I'll secure thy rear!
Defend thyself in front!——O Nathos! Nathos!
Seiz'd! torn!—Deliver me!——'Tis death I
want.

NATHOS, (*turning to her, and killing some.*)

What shall I do? Is there no other way?
Forgive me, my Darthula!——O forgive me!
[*Stabs her.*

DARTHULA, (*falling.*)

I thank thee love! 'Twas kindly done!——
·Farewell!

SOLDIERS, (*behind.*)

The Lady!

SECOND SOLDIER.

O the Lady!

THIRD SOLDIER.

She is dead!

NA·

NATHOS.

There's nothing now in life!

CAIRBAR.

Hold! Strike not yet.
He muft be tortur'd for this dreadful murder!
Carry the body hence! Be it thy care,
Old Bard, to fee it decently interr'd.

NATHOS.

Doft thou ftill hover o'er the head of Nathos,
And chide this long delay? Or doft thou
    fhrink
From thy loth'd murderer?—I murder'd thee!
Cairbar! if thou didft love Darthula, ftrike:
'Twas I that murder'd her!——Revenge her
    death!

CAIRBAR.

No! My refentment better is indulg'd,
To fee thee live, and thus torment thyfelf.

NATHOS.

Think'ft thou I have a grov'ling foul like
    thine,

To

'To bear for life remorſe and infamy?
No! 'tis determin'd! I will fall with her!
And in my falling—thus avenge our wrongs.

*(Breaks in upon them with his ſword and
ſhield, kills two or three, and puts them in
confuſion.——Shouting and noiſe of fighting
without.)*

*Enter ſoldiers calling, "Fingal, Oſcar, Oſſian,
Nathos, Uſnoth."——Cairbar's party flying,
leaves him expoſed.*

NATHOS, *(running at Cairbar, who endeavours
to get off.)*

Die, king of cruelty! Now let the world
In ſafety live! Darthula, thou'rt reveng'd!

CAIRBAR, *(after he is down.)*

Curſe on th' ignoble arm by which I fall!

NATHOS.

Ha! ſpeak'ſt thou ſtill? Take that to make
thee ſure.
Take that for Çormac;——and for Fruthil
this!

But

But, were thy lives as num'rous as thy hairs,
They all were far too little for Darthula.
                              [*Stabbing him often.*
Come all ye spirits dispossest by him
Of your fair dwellings! come, in vengeance,
      come,
And drag his cursed ghost to Torture's den!
Thither I'll soon pursue.——

SOLDIERS, (*shouting.*)

            Ho, Nathos! Usnoth, ho!

NATHOS.

My father! Oh! 'twill break his good old
      heart.

Enter Usnoth and soldiers.

A SOLDIER.

'Twas here the enemy surrounded him.

USNOTH.

Dead bodies here! Come forward with the
      lights!
O Nathos! art thou here?

                              NA-

NATHOS.

I am, my father.

USNOTH.

My Nathos ſtill is left to bleſs my age!
How is it with my ſon?

NATHOS.

I've ſlain the tyrant.
See where the curſed murderer's body lies!

USNOTH.

Bear the deteſted object from our ſight!
I fear, my ſon, thou haſt receiv'd ſome hurt.
Elſe wherefore doſt thou groan and bite thy
lip?
Why ſtare ſo wild? Why thus dejected
frown,
When thou ſhouldſt ſmile at the proud ty-
rant's fall,
And wear the chearful face of victory?

NATHOS.

The voice of victory ſhall chear no more!
Wounded I am not; but in mind much hurt!
I'll

I'll fmile no more till I am with Darthula!——

I murder'd her!——I've murder'd all my
fmiles!——

USNOTH.

What! Murder'd! Who? Darthula! Thou,
thyfelf?

NATHOS.

To free her from the murderer's threaten'd
force;
The brutal luft of his detefted paffion,
No means feem'd poffible.——In rafh de-
fpair
I ftruck: 'Twas her requeft.——O fool, rafh
fool!——
Oh, had you come before Darthula dy'd!—
Had I delay'd till now, we had been hap-
py!

USNOTH.

Be comforted, my fon! Some favouring
pow'r

Hhh

May make thee happy where thou dar'ft not
hope.

NATHOS.

I have no hopes!——What can I hope?——
What pow'r
Can bring my love, my murder'd fair, to
life?
What can extirpate from my memory
The fad reflection that I kill'd my love?——
I cannot live!——My father! O my father!

USNOTH.

Your forrows cannot call her back from
death.

NATHOS.

I fent her but before, to follow her.

USNOTH.

What means my fon?——Thou wilt not
flay thyfelf?

NATHOS.

I've flain already dearer than myfelf!

Dar-

Darthula!——There I fuffer'd worfe than
    death!——
Eafier I could have torn my vitals out!——
I promifed! I muft, I muft perform!
Yes, my Darthula! I will come to thee!——

USNOTH.

O Nathos! Nathos! could'ft thou kill thy
    father?
But furely killing him were not fo bad,
As thus refigning him to what is worfe.

NATHOS.

To leave thee, O my father, racks my
    foul!
But my fad life could never comfort thee!
Sorrow, remorfe, defpair, will ftill infeft
My future days!——Darthula waits too long.

USNOTH.

And muft thy wretched father die de-
    priv'd
Of all his fons!——Lay firft this hoary head
Peaceful to flumber in the filent grave!

NATHOS.

NATHOS.

She faid her foul would hover o'er my
head,
Till mine came from my breaft! Doft thou
not fee her;
For fhe is near!—Doft thou not hear her
voice,
In the low accents of unorgan'd ghofts,
Reproaching me with this unkind delay?

USNOTH.

Muft I be now bereft of every joy,
Of every comfort, in the wane of life?

NATHOS.

She gently thank'd me for the murd'ring
wound!
Her laft fad looks invited me away!
She in her calm farewell appear'd affur'd,
That to her fpirit mine fhould fhortly come!

USNOTH.

Let pity for thy wretched father force

That

That dang'rous weapon from thy defperate
    hand.

NATHOS, (*throwing away the fword.*)

Hence, ufelefs inftrument, I need thee
    not!
I'll refolutely grow to this cold earth,
             [*Cafting himfelf down.*
Until my rotten limbs mix with the foil,
And my freed fpirit to Darthula rife.

USNOTH.

Thou laft, thou ever deareft of my fons!
Let me die firft! Let me not live to fee
All, all my family, extinct before me!

Enter Darthula, Althan.

DARTHULA.

How can he live? Ye only flatter me!
A thoufand lances at his breaft I faw!
A thoufand harden'd murderers wielded
    them!
                    USNOTH.

USNOTH.

Was Colla's daughter lovelier than fhe?

DARTHULA.

Bring me where bleeding yet his body lies,
And with my tears I'll wafh his blood away!

USNOTH.

What lady's this, fo mournful and fo fair?

DARTHULA.

There!—O my Nathos! Do I fee thee
    thus?
Thou died for me!——I will be with thee
    foon!
Wherefore, O wherefore did ye bring me
    back
To life? Detefted life!—Oh had I dy'd
We had ere this for ever been united!
We fhall be foon united!—I will cling
To thy yet warm, but faft-corrupting corfe!
And on thy bloody bofom fleep for ever!

NATHOS.

NATHOS, *(raising his head.)*

- I'come, my love! I hear diftinct thy voice!
When fhall I fee thy lovely, lovely fpirit?

DARTHULA.

He fpeaks! Art thou indeed alive, O Nathos?

NATHOS, *(rifing.)*

I fee thee plainly now! my dear Darthula!

DARTHULA.

He lives! he lives!

[*She faints.*

NATHOS.

What dear delufion's this?
I thought fhe liv'd, I thought fhe fpoke to
me!
I am diftracted! Let me think fo ftill!
And there is joy in everlafting madnefs!

AL-

ALTHAN.

She lives, and foon will rife to life and
thee,

NATHOS.

Why do ye mock me? Is it well my
friends,
To flatter thus a poor delirious wretch?
How can fhe live? Did I not murder her?

ALTHAN.

The ftroke came from a lover's arm, too
light
To reach the feat of life.—She fainted then,
As now fhe does.—The tyrant thought her
dead,
And gave to me the care of burying her.
She'll foon revive! The wound is free from
danger.

USNOTH.

Now fhe recovers! Stand afide, my fon,
Left

Left the furprife fhould prove too powerful
for her.

DARTHULA.

He is not here!——Ah! was it all a
dream?
I thought I faw my Nathos lying dead;
And when I fpoke he ftarted into life!

ALTHAN.

It was no dream, Darthula!——Nathos
lives!
Cairbar is flain!——Thou haft no more to
fear!
Prepare thyfelf to meet immediate joy!

DARTHULA.

If he's alive, he bleeds in deadly wounds!
Elfe wherefore would he leave Darthula
now?

NATHOS.

Left he again deftroy that lovely form!—
May I approach? May I come to thy arms?
Welcome from death, to endlefs love and
joy.

USNOTH.

USNOTH.

O brighteft happinefs, from darkeft forrow!
I fhall rejoice in my declining years,
And fee the children of my Nathos ftill!

NATHOS.

See, my Darthula! See my father here!
He almoft finks beneath excefs of joy!
'Twas he reftrain d me; elfe defpair had fent
  me
Ere this to feek thee in the fhades of death;
And curs'd thy waking with a dreadful
  fcene.

DARTHULA.

My overflowing heart can fcarce contain
Thefe floods of joy: And yet I fhudder ftill,
To think how near impatience had undone
  us.

ALTHAN.

When adverfe fortune deals her fharpeft
  blows,
With refolution firm, ye brave, oppofe!
      Though

Though deep the wounds, though th' anguiſh
  be ſevere,
Still ſtruggle bravely; ſtill with patience
  bear !
Sink not, deſponding, under ſtrokes of grief;
But with true fortitude expect relief:
For ſorrow's ſtorms in time themſelves de-
  ſtroy,
And brighter from their clouds ſhines the ſuc-
  ceeding joy !

THE END.

www.ingramcontent.com/pod-product-compliance
Lightning Source LLC
Chambersburg PA
CBHW022009110726
47901CB00006B/1458